Ray to

Thank you for
loving Jesus. Let
him carry you through
All Things

Shay

All of Me

of

*Living as a Tried and Tested
Proven Disciple*

SHIRLEY MOSES

Contents

Acknowledgments

I would first like to thank Truman, my husband, who has spent many hours praying for my writing. He never allowed me to give up on my dream and encouraged me to continue trusting God. You are the love of my life, Truman!

I am especially grateful to Kathy Dophied and Linda Lesniewski; both spent numerous hours reading and editing my writing. Through all of this we have developed a kindred spirit that is so dear to me.

Dr. Jim Wolfe, who has been my friend and pastor, is due my sincerest gratitude for all the support and encouragement he gave so freely to make this writing possible.

My special friend, Judy Van Hooser, has encouraged and prayed for me, all the while taking a journey with me I will never forget. I love you, Chickadee!

Above all, I thank God for guiding me in the writing of this Bible study. Lord, may this bring You honor and glory and help guide Your women to become Proven Disciples.

With a grateful heart to all,

Shirley Moses

Meet the Author

Shirley Moses

Her passion for guiding women to walk with Jesus prompted Shirley to start Beyond the Call Ministries, which led her to speaking at women's conferences nationwide. Shirley has served as speaker, trainer and author for LifeWay Christian Resources. Shirley is a contributor to *Transformed Lives: Taking Women's Ministry to the Next Level* by *LifeWay Christian Resources* and has co-authored *Heart Friends*. She served as Women's Ministry Consultant for the Southern Baptists of Texas Convention for ten years and served as the Director of Women's Ministry State Leadership Team. Shirley and Truman live on a ranch in North Texas.

Introduction

Welcome!

Whether you've been a Christian for many years or just beginning your journey as a new believer, this study will help you grow as a committed follower of Christ.

Jesus Christ said, "Come follow me." Never underestimate the importance of this call. It's changed my life from despair and disillusionment to one filled with hope and joy. Many Christians struggle with following Christ with their all. They're afraid to say, "Jesus, here's 'all of me.'" I understand. I also wanted complete control of every aspect of my life. When I made the decision to submit fully to Jesus Christ's Lordship of my life, I discovered a growing desire to live more consistently for Him. With time, He became the *lover of my soul*. Even though I didn't know how to navigate this journey, God sent a woman to guide me. Without discipleship, I might have missed the joy of fully living for Christ.

As we grow in our relationship with our Savior, certain characteristics and behaviors naturally develop, like spending time in prayer, studying God's Word and allowing the Holy Spirit to influence our words and actions to glorify God. It's possible to journey through *All of Me* by yourself, but sharing the experience with a small group or pairing with a "discipleship mentor" increases the impact it can have on your life.

Resources for small groups or one-on-one discipleship mentoring are available to download at www.beyondthecallministries.org.

The Journey

All of Me offers eight weeks of study. Each week includes four days of study with the fifth day set aside for small group or one-on-one time with a discipleship mentor for reflection. Consider meeting face-to-face over coffee, through FaceTime, or by sharing the study digitally.

The only thing you'll need is a notebook for capturing your thoughts or things you'll want to share with your mentor.

God has been waiting for you to take this step of faith, so let's get started!

The Disciple's Call

WEEK ONE

Believing and Belonging
Overview

We begin this first week thinking through the basics of what it means to *believe* in Christ as your Savior and to *belong* to Him forever. We'll observe Jesus' encounter with a man who wanted to know this very thing—*what it means to believe and belong to Jesus*.

Our passage this week is John 3:1–18.

> Now there was a Pharisee, a man named Nicodemus who was a member of the Jewish ruling council. **²**He came to Jesus at night and said, "Rabbi, we know that you are a teacher who has come from God. For no one could perform the signs you are doing if God were not with him."
>
> **³**Jesus replied, "Very truly I tell you, no one can see the kingdom of God unless they are born again."
>
> **⁴**"How can someone be born when they are old?" Nicodemus asked. "Surely they cannot enter a second time into their mother's womb to be born!"

⁵Jesus answered, "Very truly I tell you, no one can enter the kingdom of God unless they are born of water and the Spirit. ⁶Flesh gives birth to flesh, but the Spirit[gives birth to spirit. ⁷You should not be surprised at my saying, 'You must be born again.' ⁸The wind blows wherever it pleases. You hear its sound, but you cannot tell where it comes from or where it is going. So it is with everyone born of the Spirit."

⁹"How can this be?" Nicodemus asked.

¹⁰"You are Israel's teacher," said Jesus, "and do you not understand these things? ¹¹Very truly I tell you, we speak of what we know, and we testify to what we have seen, but still you people do not accept our testimony. ¹²I have spoken to you of earthly things and you do not believe; how then will you believe if I speak of heavenly things? ¹³No one has ever gone into heaven except the one who came from heaven— the Son of Man. ¹⁴Just as Moses lifted up the snake in the wilderness, so the Son of Man must be lifted up, ¹⁵that every- one who believes may have eternal life in him."

¹⁶For God so loved the world that he gave his one and only Son, that whoever believes in him shall not perish but have eternal life. ¹⁷For God did not send his Son into the world to condemn the world, but to save the world through him. ¹⁸Whoever believes in him is not condemned, but whoever does not believe stands condemned already because they have not believed in the name of God's one and only Son.

I've found simple outlines helpful for grasping the truths in a passage of scripture. Here's one for John 3:1–18. See if it helps you with the big picture!

John 3:1–18 Outlined

I. The Meeting (Who and When) verses 1–2
    a. Nicodemus—a Pharisee
    b. Jesus—a Rabbi
    c. Night
II. Topic of Conversation—eternal life (What) verses 3–8
III. Lesson #1, You must be born again (What) verses 3–8
    a. Born of water
    b. Born of the Spirit (How)
IV. Lesson #2, Jesus is the Messiah (Who) verses 9–18
    a. He testifies about the truth
    b. He descended and ascended
    c. He gives eternal life to everyone who believes
    d. He is God's only Son

Week One, Day One
The Meeting

Nicodemus, an influential religious Jew, sought out Jesus. Nicodemus must have found real courage to initiate this meeting since Pharisees were angry and condescending to Jesus. Imagine the strong stirring in his heart that allowed him to overcome peer pressure and fear of losing religious status in pursing this one-on-one encounter.

Do you face this same pressure or know someone who allows pressure from family, friends or co-workers to keep them from seeking Jesus? Stop and pray right now, asking the Father to give them or yourself the courage to draw near Him regardless of outside pressures.

Another aspect of this nighttime meeting is the unfolding of Nicodemus' personal story. Two thousand years later we're still learning from *his* encounter with Jesus, just as others can learn from *ours* today! Each believer has a significant and unique experience. I've shared my story of seeking and finding Jesus. As you read it, begin thinking about your own!

Shirley's Snippets

I grew in an area of town where every house was a fixer upper. Our small home needed propping up and patching up. Even though my parents had no interest in God, my grandmother did. She'd take all ten grandchildren to a small church in walking distance from her house. After my parents divorced, we moved away from my grandmother and that little church.

I eventually married, moved to California and lived what appeared to be the good life. We had a new house, new cars, fashionable clothes, expensive jewelry and an active social life. I believed in God but had been too busy living life *my* way to give Him a second thought. God had not forgotten me, though, and knew exactly when I would turn my heart toward Him.

When my husband and I moved back to the country in Texas, my need for friends drew me to church. One Sunday I felt a stirring in my heart so strong nothing could have held me in my seat. (I learned later it was the Holy Spirit.) I quickly went to speak to the pastor and received Jesus into my life. The Holy Spirit had worked in my heart, and I responded. The very next Sunday, the pastor baptized both my husband and me into the family of God, and the whole focus of our lives began to change.

Jot It Down

What's your story? Spend a few minutes writing how you came to believe and belong to Jesus. This is *your* story. It's significant because it originated with God. You'll be sharing it with your discipleship mentor (DM) or small group. Enjoy your time of reflection. I've prayed this will be a sweet time for you with Jesus.

Week One, Day Two
The Rebirth

Now there was a Pharisee, a man named Nicodemus who was a member of the Jewish ruling council. ²He came to Jesus at night and said, "Rabbi, we know that you are a teacher who has come from God. For no one could perform the signs you are doing if God were not with him."

³Jesus replied, "Very truly I tell you, no one can see the kingdom of God unless they are born again."

⁴"How can someone be born when they are old?" Nicodemus asked. "Surely they cannot enter a second time into their mother's womb to be born!"

⁵Jesus answered, "Very truly I tell you, no one can enter the kingdom of God unless they are born of water and the Spirit. ⁶Flesh gives birth to flesh, but the Spirit gives birth to spirit. ⁷You should not be surprised at my saying, 'You must be born again.' ⁸The wind blows wherever it pleases. You hear its sound, but you cannot tell where it comes from or where it is going. So it is with everyone born of the Spirit" (John 3:1–8).

Being born again, Jesus says, is not a human endeavor. It is orchestrated by the Holy Spirit, not by human works. Notice how Nicodemus asked real questions about a very important topic. As a ruler of the

Jews, Nicodemus felt in charge and in control. The idea of a rebirth obviously meant releasing control. We too released control of our lives when we came to Him for salvation, and we must release control when we choose to follow Him as our *Lord, not just our Savior.*

Jot It Down

> Do you have a difficult time releasing control? I do! Identify areas you find it difficult to yield to Christ and consider discussing them with your DM or small group. Most importantly, discuss them with Jesus.

> Nicodemus stood at a crossroads. We see his hesitation in entering into an exclusive relationship with Him. What are you holding onto that keeps you from a sold-out relationship with Jesus?

What a special opportunity this is to join Nicodemus in his journey to discover what it means to believe and belong. Try not to hurry through these reflective questions. Tell God how much it means to you that He chose you through the work of the Holy Spirit. Tomorrow, we'll see how Jesus taught Nicodemus another lesson about accessing all that the Kingdom has for followers.

Week One, Day Three
Jesus the Messiah (Promised One)

Today we'll watch Nicodemus struggle with letting go of something else—of all he'd expected to find in the promised one, the Messiah. Nicodemus' academic accomplishments earned the title Jesus gave him—Israel's teacher. Let's review verses 9–18 and notice their conversation.

9"How can this be?" Nicodemus asked.

10"You are Israel's teacher," said Jesus, "and do you not understand these things? 11Very truly I tell you, we speak of what we know, and we testify to what we have seen, but still you people do not accept our testimony. 12I have spoken to you of earthly things and you do not believe; how then will you believe if I speak of heavenly things? 13No one has ever gone into heaven except the one who came from heaven— the Son of Man. 14Just as Moses lifted up the snake in the wilderness, so the Son of Man must be lifted up, 15that everyone who believes may have eternal life in him."

16For God so loved the world that he gave his one and only Son, that whoever believes in him shall not perish but have eternal life. 17For God did not send his Son into the world to condemn the world, but to save the world through him. 18Whoever believes in him is not condemned, but whoever does not believe stands condemned already because they have not believed in the name of God's one and only Son.

Did you notice that Nicodemus asked Jesus the same question twice? He asks, "How can these things be?" It reminds me of my toddler's attitude. Her favorite words were "No! I can!" That's the challenge Nicodemus faced—overconfidence. We often face this same issue, but Jesus consistently gets us back on track. He certainly has with me.

Nicodemus also struggled with his problem of unbelief (John 3:11–12). Jesus recognized this from the beginning and wanted to guide him to genuine belief. As I reflect on this conversation, I marvel at how patient Jesus was with me as I moved slowly toward the truth about who He was. What a loving God we have!

Jot It Down

- What had Nicodemus based his beliefs upon?
- What was Jesus asking him to trust now? Notice the solution Jesus offered for unbelief in verses 16–18.

> *16For God so loved the world that he gave his one and only Son, that whoever believes in him shall not perish but have eternal life. 17For God did not send his Son into the world to condemn the world, but to save the world through him. 18Whoever believes in him is not condemned, but whoever does not believe stands condemned already because they have not believed in the name of God's one and only Son.*

- What did Jesus tell Nicodemus about believing?
- When you first came to Jesus, was belief a problem for you at any point? Would any other portion of their conversation have caused issues for you? Does it still raise questions? Discuss it with your DM.

> Paul writes in 1 Corinthians 2:4: "My message and my preaching were not with wise and persuasive words, but with a demonstration of the Spirit's power." Do you recall a time when you became aware of the Holy Spirit's power in your life as a new believer?

This passage helps us understand God's perspective on salvation and our individual belief. Remember day two's summary—you are chosen, redeemed and loved? Verse 16 reminds us of this foundational truth, *For God loved the world in this way: He gave His One and Only Son, so that everyone who believes in Him will not perish but have eternal life.* God has chosen us to be part of His family. Nicodemus had to accept this truth that redemption came from the Son of Man who gave His life on the cross because God loved the world. He wasn't able to simply follow the law and earn his own way. Chosen. Redeemed. Loved.

Verse 4 says the Spirit must be involved for us to understand truth. Nicodemus had a lot to think about. The Seeker came in secret and to meet someone who would one day be his Savior, but this man's story does not end here. There's much more. See you on day four!

Week One, Day Four
From Fearful to Follower

Not all of the stories in God's Word have a happy ending; however, this one makes me want to stand up and shout!

Notice in John 19:38–42 each person and the part he played in the burial of Jesus—Joseph of Arimathea and Nicodemus.

> *38Later, Joseph of Arimathea asked Pilate for the body of Jesus. Now Joseph was a disciple of Jesus, but secretly because he feared the Jewish leaders. With Pilate's permission, he came and took the body away. 39He was accompanied by Nicodemus, the man who earlier had visited Jesus at night. Nicodemus brought a mixture of myrrh and aloes, about seventy-five pounds. 40Taking Jesus' body, the two of them wrapped it, with the spices, in strips of linen. This was in accordance with Jewish burial customs. 41At the place where Jesus was crucified, there was a garden, and in the garden a new tomb, in which no one had ever been laid. 42Because it was the Jewish day of Preparation and since the tomb was nearby, they laid Jesus there* (John 19:38–42).

When we last read about Nicodemus in John 3, he was struggling with unbelief. He must have continued to keep tabs on Jesus and to follow the stirrings of his heart because Nicodemus shows back up in John 19.

Joseph also followed the leading of his heart. In John 19, we read that Joseph had been a secret disciple of Jesus. Why did he follow in secret? In Luke 23:50-51, we discover he served as a member of the Sanhedrin council. *Now there was a man named Joseph, a member of the Council, a good and upright man....* If other members had discovered Joseph was a follower of Jesus, they would have dismissed him from the council. Sounds familiar?

It's wonderful to see how God can move followers from fearful to faithful! These two men, Joseph and Nicodemus, openly identify as followers of Jesus as they tenderly remove Jesus from the cross. Joseph left his fear of what others might do and went boldly to Pilate to ask for Jesus' body (see Mark 15:43). No longer afraid, these men transformed into faithful followers. That is what an encounter with Jesus can also do for us as He brings us out of the shadows to follow faithfully.

Do any of these situations describe yours?

- I have friendships that draw me away from following Jesus faithfully.
- Social pressures me to keep my relationship with Jesus a secret.
- I have family members who are not followers of Jesus and don't want me to be one either.
- Many of my associates do not believe in God or Jesus.
- My work requires me to keep Jesus out of my workplace.

There will always be those people who try to discourage us from following Jesus, but we must resist discouragement. Jesus will always provide what we need to continue to walk with Him. Discuss this with your DM and ask for her wisdom about openly living for Jesus. When you're tempted to live as a secret follower, remember Joseph and Nicodemus. God transformed them into faithful followers. He can do the same for you!

Discipleship is about following, but it's also about ministry. Both of these men used what they had to offer to care for their Savior. That's authentic ministry—using what you have for the benefit of others. It might be your time, your money or your possessions. Joseph eventually furnished the linen bandages and his personal tomb (Matt. 27:59). Nicodemus provided the expensive aromatic spices. Both invested not only what they had but also their presence.

Here's a summary of the key points we've covered:

- Rebirth is the work of the Holy Spirit, not by our own efforts.
- The Son of Man died on the cross for my sins.
- God loved the world in this way: He gave His One and Only Son so that everyone who believes in Him will not perish but have eternal life.
- We are loved by God long before we believe and belong.
- His love calls us to respond by following Him.

I hope you've already scheduled a time to meet with your DM or small group. Next week we'll examine what it means to follow Christ. I encourage you to journal some of your thoughts. It'll provide an additional level of growth. Here's a simple way to approach it.

Journaling Growth

- Key thoughts
- Commandment or example for me to obey/follow
- Personal application
- Pray requests for myself or others
- Things I want to discuss with my DM

The Disciple's Path

WEEK TWO

Overview

Last week we talked about what it means to believe in Jesus as the Son of God and what it means to actually belong to Him as a child of God—believing and belonging.

When Jesus says, "Follow me," he was issuing a personal invitation. Jesus invites those who have believed and now belong to Him to follow him as sheep follow their Shepherd. This week you'll glimpse the heart of Jesus, the Good Shepherd, and the importance of following Him.

We'll focus on John 10:1–13.

> "Very truly I tell you Pharisees, anyone who does not enter the sheep pen by the gate, but climbs in by some other way, is a thief and a robber. ²The one who enters by the gate is the shepherd of the sheep. ³The gatekeeper opens the gate for him, and the sheep listen to his voice. He calls his own sheep by name and leads them out. ⁴When he has brought out all his own, he goes on ahead of them, and his sheep follow him because they know his voice. ⁵But they will never follow a stranger; in fact, they will run away from him because they do not recognize a stranger's voice." ⁶Jesus used this figure

of speech, but the Pharisees did not understand what he was telling them.

7Therefore Jesus said again, "Very truly I tell you, I am the gate for the sheep. 8All who have come before me are thieves and robbers, but the sheep have not listened to them. 9I am the gate; whoever enters through me will be saved. They will come in and go out, and find pasture. 10The thief comes only to steal and kill and destroy; I have come that they may have life, and have it to the full."

11"I am the good shepherd. The good shepherd lays down his life for the sheep. 12The hired hand is not the shepherd and does not own the sheep. So when he sees the wolf coming, he abandons the sheep and runs away. Then the wolf attacks the flock and scatters it. 13The man runs away because he is a hired hand and cares nothing for the sheep."

A Simplified Outline

I. The Good Shepherd, the sheep and the thief (verses 1–6)
    A. The thief
        a. Doesn't enter by the door
        b. Sheep don't recognize his voice
        c. Sheep run away
    B. The Shepherd
        a. Enters by the door
        b. Sheep recognize His voice
        c. He goes ahead of them
        d. Sheep follow the Shepherd
II. Explanation of the parable (verses 7–13)
    A. Jesus is the door
        a. Sheep enter through Jesus

    b. Sheep are saved through Jesus

    c. Sheep find pasture through Jesus

  B. Jesus is the Good Shepherd

    a. He gives abundant life

    b. He lays down his life for the sheep

  C. The thief

    a. Steals

    b. Kills

    c. Destroys

  D. The hired man

    a. Is not the shepherd

    b. Doesn't own the sheep

    c. Leaves the sheep when the wolf comes

    d. Doesn't care about the sheep

Week Two, Day One
The Shepherd and the Sheep

Sheep—dirty, smelly and not so smart. That's what comes to mind when I think of sheep. I much prefer the big-eyed lambs on Christmas cards! By the end of the week, though, I'm confident you'll be thrilled to be known as one of Jesus' sheep!

Shirley's Snippets

A sweet lady, Maggie, timidly said, "As I dropped off to sleep last night, God brought you to mind and this story. I once visited a friend's sheep ranch and watched a herder trying to move sheep and their babies from their birthing corral to a new pasture. A muddy passageway divided the two areas. We watched as he hit the sheep with a long stick in an attempt to drive them across that muddy water. Things weren't going well. Just as he got each ewe across the water, she'd turn back. Suddenly my friend shouted, 'Stop hitting the sheep!' and headed to the front of the flock. Once there, she simply stepped across the water and into the pasture. Surprisingly, one by one, the sheep began to follow her across the water and into their new home." Maggie added, "This incident reminded of John 10:3, ...*the sheep hear his voice. He calls his own sheep by name and leads them out.*"

The Need for a Shepherd

Have you ever lost your way and needed help? I often do, even with GPS. Sometimes I ignore instructions and go the direction I choose—and usually end up lost. The same thing happens in my life when I follow my self-will rather than God's leadership. Nothing seems to turn out like I want it to.

Sometimes we need our Shepherd to protect us from within, from ourselves. The prophet Jeremiah tells us an important truth and then asks us a question, "*The heart is deceitful above all things and beyond cure. Who can understand it?*" (Jeremiah 17:9) Think about it a moment—the heart is more deceitful than anything else.

We also need protection from outside. John 10:1 records Jesus' warning, "*I assure you, anyone who doesn't enter the sheep pen by the door but climbs in some other way is a thief and a robber.*" Without the help of our Shepherd, our hearts and others will mislead us. Take time to reflect upon these two verses about ways the Good Shepherd leads us.

Note how the Shepherd protects our hearts in these passages:

Create in me a pure heart, O God, and renew a steadfast spirit within me (Psalm 51:10).

I have hidden your word in my heart that I might not sin against you (Psalm 119:11).

Jot It Down

- Think of a situation where you didn't know what to do yet you found your way because you looked to God to show you.
- How did the Good Shepherd's voice guide you?
- End this day with a heart check, asking the Good Shepherd to reveal anything that keeps you from following Him. This is an important step. Take the time to record your thoughts to share with your DM or small group. Let their prayers for you be a source of encouragement.

Week Two, Day Two
Companionship with Jesus

Yesterday we discovered how deceitful the heart can be without God's direction. Today we will investigate how consistently following Jesus produces a relationship that begins to feel more and more like a dependable travel-mate, a companion. This type of gentle companionship also shows up among Christian friendships. We often use the word "fellowship." I love that word and how it describes what Jesus wants for our relationship with Him.

Let's review today's passage:

> *The one who enters by the gate is the shepherd of the sheep. The gatekeeper opens the gate for him, and the sheep listen to his voice. He calls his own sheep by name and leads them out. When he has brought out all his own, he goes on ahead of them, and his sheep follow him because they know his voice. But they will never follow a stranger; in fact, they will*

run away from him because they do not recognize a stranger's voice (John 10:2–5).

Shirley's Snippets

I live in a small country town in Texas. When I first arrived from California, I felt exposed by the everyone-knows-your-business culture. After a while, though, what initially felt like intrusion began to feel more like personal concern. When we follow Jesus our Shepherd, He establishes a concerned relationship through the time we spend with Him. As this relationship grows in depth and intimacy, it'll extend to those around us. Jesus cares about those too.

Within this developing companionship, you might experience times when you feel conviction about areas He wants you to address—friendships, activities, behaviors etc. Perhaps you'll feel it's time to repair a broken relationship. The Holy Spirit will bring the specific event that caused the rift to our minds and guide us in how to seek healing.

What growth would you like to see in your own relationships a year from now? Be specific. If you desire growth, God will guide you. When you sit down with God's Word, the Holy Spirit will help your heart understand the truths recorded there. You'll begin to learn the sound of the Shepherd's voice. In John 10: 2–5, Jesus clearly explained what His guidance looked like. His "voice," His leadership in our lives, is a direct result of following Christ and experiencing companionship/fellowship/friendship with Him. Jesus spoke clearly, "...the sheep follow Him because they recognize His voice."

Reflect on these verses that guide our hearts to seek God and to discover how He communicates to us through his Word.

I meditate on your precepts and consider your ways (Psalm 119:15).

Open my eyes that I may see wonderful things in your law (Psalm 119:18).

Cause me to understand the way of your precepts, that I may meditate on your wonderful deeds (Psalm 119:27).

Give me understanding so that I may keep your law and obey it with all my heart (Psalm 119:34).

He Knows Us and Leads Us

As we learn to fellowship with Jesus, we not only learn the sound of His voice, but we also discover He knows us by name! In fact, He has your name written in two very important places.

See, I have engraved you on the palms of my hands (Isaiah 49:16).

Nothing impure will ever enter it, nor will anyone who does what is shameful or deceitful, but only those whose names are written in the Lamb's book of life (Revelation 21:27).

Knowing where God has written your name shows the intimate connection Jesus wants when He invites you to follow Him. God provides many more benefits to companionship with Jesus. Jesus says in John 10:3, "... *the sheep listen to his voice. He calls his own sheep by name and leads them out.*" We'll be learning more about how He leads us.

I've discovered, though, that as confidence in His leading grew so did a sense of boldness. Remember Maggie's story about her friend leading the sheep across the water? The sheep overcame their fear of crossing the water because they had someone to go before them.

God's Word speaks often about fear. I really like Psalm 118:6 in the Message translation: "*Pushed to the wall, I called to God; from the wide open spaces, he answered. God's now at my side and I'm not afraid; who would dare lay a hand on me?*"

God's presence can bring us courage. We no longer have to be afraid—of anything. Seek out this amazing companionship with your Savior and Lord as you follow Him. Watch with wonder how He leads and the surprising qualities He'll begin developing in your life.

Jot It Down
- Recall a time Jesus has led you through challenging times.
- What do you fear?

Week Two, Day Three
Following in Confidence and in Freedom

Jesus portrays himself as the door of the sheep pen. John 10:6 says that *the Pharisees did not understand what he was telling them.* Because of this, Jesus speaks again using a different analogy. Fortunately, He does the same with us, He will not quit until we have enough understanding to move forward as we follow Him.

> Therefore Jesus said again, "Very truly I tell you, I am the gate for the sheep. All who have come before me are thieves and robbers, but the sheep have not listened to them. I am the gate; whoever enters through me will be saved" (John 10:7–9).

The Gate

The gate in this analogy provides both an entrance and an exit for the sheep. Other translations call it the "door." Jesus is the door to our salvation as well as our source of protection from things that can harm us. He can shut out what threatens us. We have the safety of His presence in the smallest details of our lives as well as the greater needs of our lives—provision. We can walk with confidence while following Him yet also rest in safety and in his protection.

Shirley's Snippets

As a new driver, I relished the feeling of freedom—going places without my parents! I heard the same reminders each time—be responsible, don't speed, be home on time. I'm sure if we'd had cell phones back then my parents would have added, "No texting and driving!"

One evening, my younger sister and I decided to go driving without permission. My sister sneaked the keys from mom's purse, then helped me push the car down the driveway so we wouldn't wake our parents when we started it. Not only did the car graze the side of the carport, it also picked up speed as it rolled toward the street before bumping the curb. The commotion awakened both my parents and the neighbors! Even though I lost my driving freedom, I did learn an important lesson.

The Good Shepherd watches over us and provides the way for our salvation, but we must make choices along the way.

Finding Good Pasture

No sheep are ever more cared for than those of the Good Shepherd, yet our hearts tempt us to look for greener pastures. Remember how much I enjoyed what I thought was the good life before meeting this wonderful Shepherd? I thought I had it all. Matthew, one of the disciples, recorded for us some of Jesus' teachings about how to enjoy the abundance our Good Shepherd promises to provide for us.

Do not store up for yourselves treasures on earth, where moths and vermin destroy, and where thieves break in and steal. But store up for yourselves treasures in heaven, where moths and vermin do not destroy, and where thieves do not break in and steal. For where your treasure is, there your heart will be also (Matthew 6:19–21).

Jot It Down

- Share with your DM a time God used a life experience to teach you an important truth about a choice God asked you to make.
- As you are learning to feel God's protective care and abundant provision, identify areas where you struggle to be content, where you're tempted to not follow your Shepherd.
- In contrast, also list the areas where God has truly supplied the deepest needs of your heart and begun the transforming work of teaching you His voice and His leading.

Week Two, Day Four
Good Shepherd or Hired Hand?

I am the good shepherd. The good shepherd lays down his life for the sheep. The hired hand is not the shepherd and does not own the sheep. So when he sees the wolf coming, he abandons the sheep and runs away. Then the wolf attacks the flock and scatters it. The man runs away because he is a hired hand and cares nothing for the sheep (John 10:11–13).

Jesus came for the purpose of providing payment for our sins and to make a way to restore our relationship with the Father. The concept of salvation has many dimensions. Jesus not only called himself the Savior but also our Shepherd. What a glorious thought to rest in. Today we want to examine another aspect of becoming a consistent, devoted, fruitful disciple—who or what we choose to put our trust in.

Your maturing walk with Christ influences both your choices and how you interpret or respond to your circumstances. If you recognize Jesus as the Good Shepherd, no matter what comes into your life, you will be okay because you are following the One who cares for you. Others may encourage and help, but they cannot satisfy the need in your heart for the Shepherd.

Shirley's Snippets

Are you a hands-on kind of woman who can tackle any problem? I'm not, but I'm great at spotting a woman who has a broken heart. We each have weaknesses and strengths. God chooses our unique design. Thankfully, He also led me to a husband who's strong in areas where I'm weak. Even though Truman gladly cares for me, he's not the true Shepherd of my heart. He doesn't have the ability to change the hard circumstances of life or transform my heart. Jesus is the only one capable of doing that, the Good Shepherd who laid down His life for me.

The parable Jesus taught in John 10 refers to the hired man as anyone who *doesn't care about the sheep.* Even though he's there during the easy times, the hired man is the first to run away when the hard times—the wolves—arrive. The sheep suffer the consequences. They're snatched and scattered. We see snatched and scattered lives all around us and wonder how they got that way. Most of us also know those feelings, the emptiness we experience when we've made the wrong choices by following the hired hand.

Culture wants to tell us what we need for happiness—the right makeup, attire or car. Culture affirms exciting careers and glamorous homes. These enticing messages direct us to trust the hired hand but don't prepare us to withstand the assault of the inevitable wolves. As we grow in our devotion to following the Lord, we must be sensitive to messages we cannot trust.

James, the half-brother of Jesus, reminds us again of this fundamental truth Jesus is discussing with the Pharisees. *Listen, my dear brothers and sisters: Has not God chosen those who are poor in the eyes of the world to be rich in faith and to inherit the kingdom he promised those who love him* (James 2:5)?

Additional Treasures

Do not love the world or anything in the world. If anyone loves the world, love for the Father is not in them (1 John 2:15).

What good will it be for someone to gain the whole world, yet forfeit their soul? Or what can anyone give in exchange for their soul (Matthew 16:26)?

Jot It Down

- What principle do I choose to make a part of my daily walk?
- How can I apply one of these truths to my life today?
- List specific instances when you were led astray by messages from culture. Spend time discussing these choices with the Lord and asking His forgiveness.

Journaling Growth

- Key thoughts
- Commandment or example for me to obey/follow
- Personal application
- Pray requests for myself or others
- Things I want to discuss with my DM

The Disciple's Devotion
WEEK THREE

Overview

God's Word contains clear instruction about the type of relationship He wants to develop with His disciples. This week, we'll examine two qualities Jesus often talked about in Scripture—His love for us, even when we sin, and our need for restoration.

This is one of those times I wish we could rock on my porch, sip sweet tea and talk at length about Jesus. Understanding God's love and how He wants it to flow through us to others is foundational to following Christ. This week's passage is found in John 21:1–17.

> Afterward Jesus appeared again to his disciples, by the Sea of Galilee. It happened this way: ²Simon Peter, Thomas (also known as Didymus), Nathanael from Cana in Galilee, the sons of Zebedee, and two other disciples were together. ³"I'm going out to fish," Simon Peter told them, and they said, "We'll go with you." So they went out and got into the boat, but that night they caught nothing.
>
> ⁴Early in the morning, Jesus stood on the shore, but the disciples did not realize that it was Jesus.
>
> ⁵He called out to them, "Friends, haven't you any fish?"

"No," they answered.

⁶He said, "Throw your net on the right side of the boat and you will find some." When they did, they were unable to haul the net in because of the large number of fish.

⁷Then the disciple whom Jesus loved said to Peter, "It is the Lord!" As soon as Simon Peter heard him say, "It is the Lord," he wrapped his outer garment around him (for he had taken it off) and jumped into the water. ⁸The other disciples followed in the boat, towing the net full of fish, for they were not far from shore, about a hundred yards. ⁹When they landed, they saw a fire of burning coals there with fish on it, and some bread.

¹⁰Jesus said to them, "Bring some of the fish you have just caught." ¹¹So Simon Peter climbed back into the boat and dragged the net ashore. It was full of large fish, 153, but even with so many the net was not torn. ¹²Jesus said to them, "Come and have breakfast." None of the disciples dared ask him, "Who are you?" They knew it was the Lord. ¹³Jesus came, took the bread and gave it to them, and did the same with the fish. ¹⁴This was now the third time Jesus appeared to his disciples after he was raised from the dead. ¹⁵When they had finished eating, Jesus said to Simon Peter, "Simon son of John, do you love me more than these?"

"Yes, Lord," he said, "you know that I love you."

Jesus said, "Feed my lambs."

¹⁶Again Jesus said, "Simon son of John, do you love me?"

He answered, "Yes, Lord, you know that I love you."

Jesus said, "Take care of my sheep."

¹⁷The third time he said to him, "Simon son of John, do you love me?"

Peter was hurt because Jesus asked him the third time, "Do you love me?" He said, "Lord, you know all things; you know that I love you."

Jesus said, "Feed my sheep."

Simplified Outline

I.   The Disciples Go Fishing (verses 1–6)
    A.   A. On their own, the disciples catch nothing.
    B.   B. Jesus gives them direction.
    C.   C. With Jesus, the disciples catch many fish.

II. The Disciples Recognize Jesus (verses 7–14)
    A.   Peter recognizes Jesus first.
    B.   The other disciples recognize Him.
    C.   Jesus and the disciples share a meal.

III. Jesus Reinstates Peter (verses 15–17)
    A.   Jesus repeats His questions.
    B.   Peter answers honestly.
    C.   Jesus directs Peter.

Week Three, Day One
Jesus Seeks Us Out

Before we examine this passage, let's think about why Peter and the disciples returned to fishing. They had gone to where they first met Jesus—the water. On the night before His arrest, Jesus encouraged the disciples to love one another because this would be how the world would know they belonged to Him. He also tried to prepare them for the difficult hours ahead.

30And when they had sung a hymn, they went out to the Mount of Olives. 31Then Jesus said to them, "You will all fall away because of me this night. For it is written, 'I will strike the shepherd, and the sheep of the flock will be scattered.' 32But after I am raised up, I will go before you to Galilee." 33Peter answered him, "Though they all fall away because of you, I will never fall away." 34Jesus said to him, "Truly, I tell you, this very night, before the rooster crows, you will deny me three times." 35Peter said to him, "Even if I must die with you, I will not deny you!" And all the disciples said the same (Matthew 26:30–35).

Nevertheless, not long after Jesus speaks these words, we find Peter sitting in the courtyard. Just as Jesus had foretold, Peter denied the Lord three times. Note the words Peter used to deny Jesus.

9Now Peter was sitting out in the courtyard, and a servant girl came to him. "You also were with Jesus of Galilee," she said.

70But he denied it before them all. "I don't know what you're talking about," he said.

71Then he went out to the gateway, where another servant girl saw him and said to the people there, "This fellow was with Jesus of Nazareth."

72He denied it again, with an oath: "I don't know the man!"

73After a little while, those standing there went up to Peter and said, "Surely you are one of them; your accent gives you away."

74Then he began to call down curses, and he swore to them, "I don't know the man!"

Immediately a rooster crowed. ⁷⁵Then Peter remembered the word Jesus had spoken: "Before the rooster crows, you will disown me three times." And he went outside and wept bitterly (Matthew 26:69–75).

What a tragedy for Peter. His guilt must have been overwhelming after he said, "I do not know this man," not once, but three times. No wonder he wanted to just go back to a familiar place where he had enjoyed fishing. Here's where this week's passage begins in John 21:3.

> ³*"I'm going out to fish," Simon Peter told them, and they said, "We'll go with you." So they went out and got into the boat, but that night they caught nothing.*
>
> *They caught nothing—until they heard a voice from the shore saying,*
>
> *"Friends, haven't you any fish?"*
>
> *"No," they answered.*
>
> ⁶*He said, "Throw your net on the right side of the boat and you will find some." When they did, they were unable to haul the net in because of the large number of fish.*

The disciples trusted Jesus enough to obey His instructions, even though they had fished all night and caught nothing. This story is less about catching fish and more about the character of Jesus and the disciples' obedience. That's true for us too.

Each time Jesus identifies Himself to us through His love, we learn to trust Him more. It's His unconditional love toward us that shows us how to love others and how to grow in our devotion to Him as disciples.

> *Surely your goodness and love will follow me*
> *all the days of my life,*

and I will dwell in the house of the Lord

forever (Psalm 23:6).

Jot It Down

- Can you think of a time when Jesus demonstrated His love for you?
- Take time to thank the Lord for this specific demonstration of His love. Ask Him to open your eyes to all the evidences of His love you've missed seeing!

Week Three, Day Two
The Pitfall of Pride

Yesterday we examined how Jesus shows Himself to us through His love. Today we will come face to face with a common struggle—pride. Go back to Day One and review Matthew 26:69–75. Jesus, the very one Peter had declared as the Christ, the Son of God, had told Peter he would deny Him. Peter, though, felt overly confident that would never happen and publicly declared his allegiance to Christ. Very shortly, Peter ended up in the high priest's courtyard and had his loyalty to Christ tested.

Shirley's Snippets

I've learned that an arrogant heart takes us to dangerous places. I taught a small women's Bible study group that had quickly grown. I truly loved those women and they knew it. We were growing together in our understanding of what it meant to become a devoted disciple of Christ. When I distributed a long list of responsibilities to the group "care leaders," they quickly let me know that I had unrealistic expectations. I had allowed pride in my own organizational skills for the group to become more important than how the women felt. It was a painful lesson to learn.

Pride traps our hearts and holds them in dark places. There will be times when we, like Peter, will deny Christ. We can deny our love of Him by the way we live, the places we go, the way we spend our money or the way we speak to others. These choices may appear to be more subtle sins than blatant pride, but the outcome remains the same—they keep us from the deep, intimate love relationship God wants for us. What's even worse is that Satan can hide these from us making them hard for us to see in ourselves.

Many of our problems result from pride's disguised work. This self-centered sin is easy to miss, because it feels like such a normal part of our everyday lives: health, careers, children, relationships, cars. Fortunately, Jesus understands the temptations that come our way. Scripture says, "He was tempted in all things. That surely included the temptation of pride."

> *15For we do not have a high priest who is unable to empathize with our weaknesses, but we have one who has been tempted in every way, just as we are—yet he did not sin. 16Let us then approach God's throne of grace with confidence, so that we may receive mercy and find grace to help us in our time of need* (Hebrews 4:115–16).

He will never scold us when we come to Him for help. Instead, He will provide what is needed to overcome—mercy, grace and His father's own power available to us through His Holy Spirit within us.

Jot It Down

- Ask the Lord to reveal any pride that needs to be addressed.

31

- What other weakness do you find yourself struggling with time-after-time—resentment, a critical spirit, erotica, envy, pride? Consider sharing one or more of these areas with your DM or small group so you can pray together about them.

Week Three, Day Three
Sin and Restoration

Yesterday we looked at Peter's pride. Today we watch Jesus restore Peter through His unconditional love. Peter surely struggled with remorse over his denial of Jesus and might have assumed their relationship was irreparably damaged. Jesus extended grace and restoration as He directed Peter through the conversation we'll examine today.

Jesus' questions guided Peter into understanding his own heart. A committed follower of Christ must not let unconfessed sin destroy intimacy/communication with Jesus. Just as Jesus questioned Peter, we can answer these same questions for ourselves. As you read through the passage, answer Jesus with, "Yes, I love you."

> [10]Jesus said to them, "Bring some of the fish you have just caught." [11]So Simon Peter climbed back into the boat and dragged the net ashore. It was full of large fish, 153, but even with so many the net was not torn. [12]Jesus said to them, "Come and have breakfast." None of the disciples dared ask him, "Who are you?" They knew it was the Lord. [13]Jesus came, took the bread and gave it to them, and did the same with the fish. [14]This was now the third time Jesus appeared to his disciples after he was raised from the dead. [15]When they had finished eating, Jesus said to Simon Peter, "Simon son of John, do you love me more than these?"

"Yes, Lord," he said, "you know that I love you."

Jesus said, "Feed my lambs."

[16]Again Jesus said, "Simon son of John, do you love me?"

He answered, "Yes, Lord, you know that I love you."

Jesus said, "Take care of my sheep."

[17]The third time he said to him, "Simon son of John, do you love me?"

Peter was hurt because Jesus asked him the third time, "Do you love me?" He said, "Lord, you know all things; you know that I love you."

Jesus said, "Feed my sheep" (John 21:10–17).

Many people wonder if the fact that Jesus asked Peter three times, *"Do you love me*?" parallels the three times Peter denied Him. Very possibly. The repeated questioning also allowed Peter to do some soul-searching and brought him to a place of true humility. Jesus often deals with us in similar ways. Jesus wants us to examine the depths of our hearts with His guidance. It requires His direction and His Holy Spirit to lead us into true confession and repentance. Peter *needed* to tell Jesus, "I love you." Jesus never leaves us in despair; He always wants to bring us back to a restored relationship with Him after we've sinned.

When you need restoration:
a. Remember how much Jesus loves you.
b. Realize the depth of your love and commitment to Jesus.
c. Acknowledge your pride.
d. Take responsibility for your actions.
e. Accept the reassurance of Jesus' forgiveness.
f. Seek Jesus' directions as you move forward.

Ask your DM or small group leader about a time when Jesus clearly walked her through these steps of restoration. Be alert to apply these steps of restoration as you continue to learn how to follow Jesus with *all of you.*

Week Three, Day Four
Feed My Sheep

Few people enjoy suffering, whether it's self-inflicted or caused by outside circumstances. We all need Jesus to step in and make us whole. Jesus longs to make us the object of His gentle love and to ease our suffering.

In this tender yet painful encounter with Jesus, Peter received more than restoration; he also received an assignment—feed my sheep. As committed disciples, God calls us to also feed His sheep, to care for the people of God. I like to call it "loving out loud!"

Loving Out Loud

In order to love our sisters and brothers in Christ, let's look at how the Bible describes love. Paul writes about it in 1 Corinthians 13:4–7.

> *Love is patient, love is kind. It does not envy, it does not boast, it is not proud. [5]It does not dishonor others, it is not self-seeking, it is not easily angered, it keeps no record of wrongs. [6]Love does not delight in evil but rejoices with the truth. [7]It always protects, always trusts, always hopes, always perseveres.*

John MacArthur points out in this passage that the Greek forms of all these properties of love are actually verbs. Paul focus more on what love does than on what it looks like. In other words, love is active rather than passive.

To help understand what active love looks like, discuss with your DM or small group leader ways to express the following kind of love in caring for others: Love is patient and kind/does not envy or boast/is not arrogant or rude/does not insist on its own way/is not easily angered or keeps records of wrongs/rejoices with the truth and bears, believes, hopes and endures all things. Don't expect to be able to instantly and perfectly express God's love well in all these areas. Spiritual maturity takes time. We must, though, begin the process of learning how to love out loud. I believe, we prove how much we love Him by how much we love other people. Do you?

Journaling Growth

- Key thoughts
- Commandment or example for me to obey/follow
- Personal application
- Pray requests for myself or others
- Things I want to discuss with my DM

The Disciple's Character
WEEK FOUR

Overview

This week we study about one of Jesus' experiences while teaching at the temple in Jerusalem. We see Him interact with the self-righteous and the broken. It's not a surprise that the broken person is a woman. Jesus never shrank from those who needed Him the most—even those who didn't know they needed Him. The author of *All the Women in the Bible* shares this concerning women Jesus met along the way. "In His journeys He conversed with at least three women who had been guilty of adultery—the woman of Samaria, the woman who came to Him in the house of Simon, and now the woman of the narrative before us. His loving kindness and tender mercy characterized His dealings with each of them."

Focal Passage

¹...but Jesus went to the Mount of Olives.

²At dawn he appeared again in the temple courts, where all the people gathered around him, and he sat down to teach them. ³The teachers of the law and the Pharisees brought in a woman caught in adultery. They made her stand before the group ⁴and said to Jesus, "Teacher, this woman was caught in the act of adultery. ⁵In the Law Moses commanded us to stone such women. Now what do you say?" ⁶They were using this question as a trap, in order to have a basis for accusing him.

But Jesus bent down and started to write on the ground with his finger. ⁷When they kept on questioning him, he straightened up and said to them, "Let any one of you who is without sin be the first to throw a stone at her." ⁸Again he stooped down and wrote on the ground.

⁹At this, those who heard began to go away one at a time, the older ones first, until only Jesus was left, with the woman still standing there. ¹⁰Jesus straightened up and asked her, "Woman, where are they? Has no one condemned you?"

¹¹"No one, sir," she said.

"Then neither do I condemn you," Jesus declared. "Go now and leave your life of sin" (John 8:1–11).

Simplified Outline

I. The trap (verses 1–6)
    A. Adulteress presented
    B. Law cited
    C. Question posed

II. Jesus' response (verses 7–8)
    A. Meaningful silence
    B. Writing on the ground
    C. Challenge: Throw the first stone

III. Jesus speaks to the adulteress (verses 9–11)
    A. They don't condemn.
    B. I don't condemn.
    C. Sin no more.

Week Four, Day One
Jesus Teaches in the Temple

Jesus came to seek and save the lost (Luke 19:10). We find Him once again in the temple seeking the lost through His teaching. Just like Jesus, we can find the lost all around us. He longs for them to turn to Him for the salvation He offers. These Jews He encountered on the temple mount sought salvation through rituals that had numbed them for many generations from seeking the one true God with all their hearts. Isaiah, an Old Testament prophet, admonishes the Jews to seek God and call out to Him.

> Seek the LORD *WHILE HE MAY BE FOUND;*
>
> *call on him while he is near.*
>
> *⁷Let the wicked forsake their ways*
>
> *and the unrighteous their thoughts.*
>
> *Let them turn to the LORD, AND HE WILL HAVE MERCY ON THEM,*
>
> *and to our God, for he will freely pardon.*
>
> *⁸"For my thoughts are not your thoughts,*
>
> *neither are your ways my ways,"*
>
> *declares the LORD.*
>
> *⁹"As the heavens are higher than the earth,*
>
> *so are my ways higher than your ways*
>
> *and my thoughts than your thoughts"* (Isaiah 55:6).

The New Testament author of Hebrews reiterates the same admonition. *"And without faith it is impossible to please God, because anyone who comes to him must believe that he exists and that he rewards those who earnestly seek him"* (Hebrews 11:6).

Jot It Down

- Record in your journal what these verses have in common with one another.

- Even with all our shortcomings, we can know His loving kindness has been extended to us as well. Write a note in your journey telling Jesus how glad you are to be a woman God loves. Don't worry about eloquent words. Seek sincerity of heart. He is worthy of our praise!

Week Four Day Two
The Accusers

Today we come face-to-face with the Pharisees and scribes. Jesus must have been so weary of these men following him watching for an opportunity to trap Him in His teaching or actions. Notice their words in John 8:4–6.

> *"Teacher," they said to Him, "this woman was caught in the act of committing adultery. In the law Moses commanded us to stone such women. So what do You say?" They asked this to trap Him, in order that they might have evidence to accuse Him.*

It's clear from these verses that these keepers of the law wanted Jesus to give an answer that would violate the Law of Moses. They hoped to charge Him with a crime. They weren't interested in this woman and her wrongdoing. They hoped to destroy Jesus' influence with the people and His credibility as a teacher of the Scriptures.

Shirley's Snippets

God used a painful life lesson to teach me how to follow Him with *all of me.* I was still a new believer when I found myself caught in a personal conflict. Several influential people accused me of offering hurtful advice to a Christian friend. Even though the accusations were false and I firmly denied the charges, I felt overwhelmed and confused. That's when I sensed the Lord saying, "Be still, Shirley, I'm with you." I immediately calmed and trusted God to vindicate me of these accusations. As always, I found Him faithful. You will find Him faithful as well to vindicate you from false accusations.

Jot It Down

- Have you ever experienced public condemnation? Jot a few sentences about the experience and your feelings about it to share with your DM.
- Reflect upon the promises found in these two verses and record your thoughts.

So do not fear, for I am with you; do not be dismayed, for I am your God. I will strengthen you and help you; I will uphold you with my righteous right hand (Isaiah 41:10).

Consider it pure joy, my brothers and sisters, whenever you face trials of many kinds... (James 1:2).

Tomorrow we'll spend time thinking about the women in this confrontation.

Week Four, Day Three
The Woman Caught in Adultery

"Teacher, this woman was caught in the act of adultery. ⁵In the Law Moses commanded us to stone such women. Now

41

what do you say?"⁶They were using this question as a trap, in order to have a basis for accusing him.

But Jesus bent down and started to write on the ground with his finger. ⁷When they kept on questioning him, he straightened up and said to them, "Let any one of you who is without sin be the first to throw a stone at her." ⁸Again he stooped down and wrote on the ground.

⁹At this, those who heard began to go away one at a time, the older ones first, until only Jesus was left, with the woman still standing there. ¹⁰Jesus straightened up and asked her, "Woman, where are they? Has no one condemned you?"

¹¹"No one, sir," she said.

"Then neither do I condemn you," Jesus declared. "Go now and leave your life of sin" (John 8:4–11).

Imagine the shame and fear this woman felt being displayed in front of the men. Most biblical scholars believe she very likely stood before them completely unclothed since she was *caught in the act of adultery.* One man had taken advantage of her and now a group of men used her in an attempt to entrap Jesus. Look closely at their accusations. *"Teacher, this woman was caught in the act of adultery. In the Law Moses commanded us to stone such women. Now what do you say?"*

Here's the law these men referenced: *You shall not commit adultery* (Exodus 20:14); *You shall not commit adultery* (Deuteronomy 5:18); *If a man commits adultery with another man's wife—with the wife of his neighbor—both the adulterer and the adulteress are to be put to death* (Leviticus 20:10).

From a legal standpoint, these men did follow the teachings of the law when they announced *she deserved to die.* Adultery means sexual relations between a married person and someone other than his or her spouse. This definition includes the man involved with the woman. The man was missing in this account. Where was he? His absence confirms this was a hastily set up attempt to use this woman's situation to entrap Jesus.

Social media provides today's "public square." Do you know someone who has experienced similar public humiliation? Have you? Take time to write a sensitive note encouraging her as a sister in Christ. If this causes personal painful memories, take time to feel the same tenderness from Jesus that He showed to this woman. He is the same loving, forgiving Savior today that He was then.

Week Four, Day Four
Jesus' Acceptance

Yesterday we observed the religious leaders' confrontation while Jesus knelt and wrote in the dirt. He now stands up and says, *"The one without sin among you should be the first to throw a stone at her"* (John 8:7).

Jesus didn't deny the woman's guilt. He used this encounter to expose the sin of the accusers. He didn't answer the Pharisees. Instead, He chose just the right moment and precisely the right words. In essence, Jesus declared them unfit to pass judgment on the woman. He knew the hearts of men and knew they too had sinned by breaking the law.

Examine Paul's words in his letter to the Roman believers.

> *You, therefore, have no excuse, you who pass judgment on someone else, for at whatever point you judge another, you are condemning yourself, because you who pass judgment do the same things. ²Now we know that God's judgment against those who do such things is based on truth. ³So when you, a mere human being, pass judgment on them and*

yet do the same things, do you think you will escape God's judgment (Romans 2:1–3)?

The law did say the woman should be stoned, but Jesus moved beyond the letter of the law. He had something else to offer this publicly disgraced woman. Look at Jesus' words in John 3:17. *For God did not send his Son into the world to condemn the world, but to save the world through him.*

The story continues:

> *Then He stooped down again and continued writing on the ground. When they heard this, they left one by one, starting with the older men. Only He was left, with the woman in the center* (John 8:7–8).

I wish I knew what Jesus wrote in the dirt, but we can only speculate. What's even more interesting, though, is that Jesus and the woman are left alone. Jesus then speaks directly to her for the first time. Note His words.

> **10** *Jesus straightened up and asked her, "Woman, where are they? Has no one condemned you?"*
>
> **11** *"No one, sir," she said.*
>
> *"Then neither do I condemn you," Jesus declared. "Go now and leave your life of sin"* (John 8:10–11).

Surely this woman felt Jesus' tenderness, compassion and forgiveness when He spoke those words. (As a side note, within the Jewish culture, the term "woman" was a respectful way of addressing her. Jesus also used "woman" when addressing his mother while she stood at the foot of the cross in John 19:26.) Also notice the final words of this passage, *Go, and from now on do not sin anymore.* Jesus not only forgave, He also told her to abandon her sinful lifestyle—another demonstration of loving direction. This story provides more than a snapshot of an encounter between Jesus and legalistic leaders. It's an amazing portrayal of Jesus liberating a woman through his mercy, wisdom and power to forgive.

Shirley's Snippets

I'd almost forgotten about the accusations I mentioned earlier this week when God revealed my resentment toward one of the accusers. I knew I needed to forgive them. I told the Lord that I'd do my part in mending our relationship if He provided an opportunity. A few days later, I recognized this individual across the store. With a pounding heart, I walked toward them. Tears from all those bottled emotions began to flow by the time I drew close. When our eyes met, their eyes also filled with tears. Right in the center of that store, we hugged and reconciled. I share this story because this marked a milestone in my spiritual journey—a milestone of obedience and acceptance of others. My willingness to do what Jesus asked me to do helped me discover what it meant to give *all of me* to my Savior—and to discover the freedom and joy that results from obedience!

A New Command

John records Jesus' new commandment for followers of Christ in John 13:34–35. *"A new command I give you: Love one another. As I have loved you, so you must love one another. By this everyone will know that you are my disciples, if you love one another."*

Jot It Down

- Is there someone you have a judgmental attitude toward?

- Ask the Lord to begin a work of changing your heart, to lead you toward a place of forgiveness. Record your prayer.
- If reconciliation needs to occur, ask the Holy Spirit to guide you in any steps He might want you to take. Record your pray for reconciliation. He'll be faithful to do just that!

Journaling Growth

- Key thoughts
- Applications to my life
- Prayer requests for family/others/myself.
- Things to discuss with my DM.

The Disciple's Confidence

WEEK FIVE

Praying with Confidence
Overview

Over the last four weeks, we've explored traits of a sold-out disciple, one who has willingly o ffered their "all" to their Savior. We've learned about how that relationship with Christ began and what your personal story looked like—*believing and belonging.* We've examined what it means to fully follow Christ as your trusted Shepherd—*following faithfully.* We've also seen how Christ calls us to not only demonstrate His love to others but be willing to accept and forgive—*accepting love.*

This week we'll learn to pray with confidence by studying how Jesus prayed. Our passage is one of my favorites. Jesus' prayed following the last meal with His disciples before they left the upper room for the Mount of Olives. By the end of the week you too will be able to enter into the presence of our Father with the heart and mind of His Son. You'll also learn to pray for yourself, those closest to you, and believers all over the world as your circles of influence expand. Discover the heart of Jesus in his "High Priestly Prayer."

After Jesus said this, he looked toward heaven and prayed:

"Father, the hour has come. Glorify your Son, that your Son may glorify you. ²For you granted him authority over all people that he might give eternal life to all those you have given him. ³Now this is eternal life: that they know you, the only true God, and Jesus Christ, whom you have sent. ⁴I have brought you glory on earth by finishing the work you gave me to do. ⁵And now, Father, glorify me in your presence with the glory I had with you before the world began.

⁶"I have revealed you to those whom you gave me out of the world. They were yours; you gave them to me and they have obeyed your word. ⁷Now they know that everything you have given me comes from you. ⁸For I gave them the words you gave me and they accepted them. They knew with certainty that I came from you, and they believed that you sent me. ⁹I pray for them. I am not praying for the world, but for those you have given me, for they are yours. ¹⁰All I have is yours, and all you have is mine. And glory has come to me through them. ¹¹I will remain in the world no longer, but they are still in the world, and I am coming to you. Holy Father, protect them by the power of your name, the name you gave me, so that they may be one as we are one. ¹²While I was with them, I protected them and kept them safe by that name you gave me. None has been lost except the one doomed to destruction so that Scripture would be fulfilled.

¹³"I am coming to you now, but I say these things while I am still in the world, so that they may have the full measure of my joy within them. ¹⁴I have given them your word and the world has hated them, for they are not of the world any more than I am of the world. ¹⁵My prayer is not that you take them out of the world but that you protect them from the evil one.

16They are not of the world, even as I am not of it. **17**Sanctify them by the truth; your word is truth. **18**As you sent me into the world, I have sent them into the world. **19**For them I sanctify myself, that they too may be truly sanctified.

20"My prayer is not for them alone. I pray also for those who will believe in me through their message, **21**that all of them may be one, Father, just as you are in me and I am in you. May they also be in us so that the world may believe that you have sent me. **22**I have given them the glory that you gave me, that they may be one as we are one—**23**I in them and you in me—so that they may be brought to complete unity. Then the world will know that you sent me and have loved them even as you have loved me.

24"Father, I want those you have given me to be with me where I am, and to see my glory, the glory you have given me because you loved me before the creation of the world.

25"Righteous Father, though the world does not know you, I know you, and they know that you have sent me. **26**I have made you known to them, and will continue to make you known in order that the love you have for me may be in them and that I myself may be in them" (John 17: 1–26).

Simplified Outline

I.   Jesus prays for Himself (verses 1–5)
    A.   Glorify your son.
    B.   May they know you and Jesus Christ, your Son.
    C.   Glorify me in your presence.
II. Jesus prays for His disciples (verses 6–19)
    A.   Protect them by the power of your name.
    B.   Protect them from the evil one.

C. Sanctify them by the truth.
III. Jesus prays for all believers (verses 20–26)
    A. That all of them may be one.
    B. May they also be in us.
    C. That they might be with him to see his glory.

Even though this is a long passage, you can see by the outline that Jesus pours out His heart covering only three basic areas. You'll discover lots of blessings by the end of the week as we explore these together!

Week Five, Day One
Jesus Prays for Himself

The goal of prayer is not to try to convince God to give us what we want. We learn, instead, to ask God for His perfect will for our lives. Notice that Jesus begins His prayer talking about His own relationship with His father. Jesus asks God to "glorify your Son" *so that* Jesus might in turn glorify His father. Oh my, how I long for God to develop within me a heart that seeks His perfect will for me. God wants that for you too—a heart that is so yielded that everything you ask for has the ultimate goal of bringing glory to your Heavenly Father. I've shared an example below when I learned to not only pray for myself but also to ask God to be glorified within my circumstances.

Shirley's Snippets

A series of extended family challenges lead me to leave a life of on-the-road-ministry so I could spend more time caring for my husband and for my own needs. As I struggled to re-envision and re-structure my world, an unexpected fall injured my back. I was asking God for patience and endurance when a painful shingles rash appeared causing me to call out to God in desperation. Soon the Holy Spirit made me aware of how independently I'd been living and how little time I'd taken for prayer and for studying His Word. This personal crisis increased the spiritual sensitivity of my heart. I discovered I truly desired God's perfect will to be accomplished through my suffering. God brought me to the place of wanting everything—all of me—to be focused on the glory of God. It was a hard lesson, but one I've never forgotten.

Jesus spoke the words recorded in John 17, just before His arrest and death on the cross. It's obvious Jesus had His heart set on glorifying God, not on His personal comfort. Perhaps you too are dealing with serious illness, pain or sorrow and feeling your own desperation. You can trust the Father. Never give up on Him. We don't face hardships alone. Sometimes it takes all the courage we have to pray, "God, I desire to bring You glory, and I will trust and accept however You choose to bring that about." The Holy Spirit will guide you and provide hope—hope that does not disappoint. May He find us faithful disciples who have set our hearts on the same goal!

> The LORD MAKES FIRM THE STEPS
> of the one who delights in him;
> though he may stumble, he will not fall,
> for the LORD UPHOLDS HIM WITH HIS HAND
> (Psalm 37:23, 24).

Tomorrow we'll learn about praying for those closest to use.

Jot It Down

- Record your most pressing concerns/struggles in your journal to discuss with your DM or small group.

Journaling Growth

Study Romans 5:1–5 and answer the following questions:

Verse 1. What has God given us through Jesus Christ?

Verse 2. As believers in Christ, to whom do we have access?

Verse 3. What can we rejoice in? What is the result?

Verse 4. What does endurance and tribulation produce?

Verse 5. What has been given to us? Who made this possible?

Week Five, Day Two
Jesus' Prayers for His Disciples

Like Jesus, we also have a circle of people close to us that we care about—family, friends, neighbors or co-workers. John 17:6–19 reveals the heart of Jesus concerning this special group.

> *⁶"I have revealed you to those whom you gave me out of the world. They were yours; you gave them to me and they have obeyed your word. ⁷Now they know that everything you have given me comes from you. ⁸For I gave them the words you gave me and they accepted them. They knew with certainty that I came from you, and they believed that you sent me. ⁹I pray for them. I am not praying for the world, but for those you have given me, for they are yours. ¹⁰All I have is yours, and all you have is mine. And glory has come to me through them. ¹¹I will remain in the world no longer, but they are still in the world, and I am coming to you. Holy Father, protect them by the power of your name, the name you gave me, so that they may be one as we are one. ¹²While I was with them, I protected them and kept them safe by that name you gave*

me. None has been lost except the one doomed to destruction so that Scripture would be fulfilled.

13"I am coming to you now, but I say these things while I am
still in the world, so that they may have the full measure of
my joy within them. 14I have given them your word and the
world has hated them, for they are not of the world any more
than I am of the world. 15My prayer is not that you take them
out of the world but that you protect them from the evil one.
16They are not of the world, even as I am not of it. 17Sanctify
them by the truth; your word is truth. 18As you sent me into
the world, I have sent them into the world. 19For them I sanctify myself, that they too may be truly sanctified."

We too can learn how to pray for those closest to our hearts. One of the
things Jesus asked the Father for was protection.

Shirley's Snippets

I once heard a story of how the American Indians equipped
their young men for adulthood. The final challenge required
a young man to spend a night alone in the woods. It was a
terrifying experience for sure. The morning light revealed,
though, that the father had been there all along watching
over his son. The story provided a special image in my mind
of how our Heavenly Father watches over us—even when
we're not aware. As believers, though, we have the benefit
of knowing our Father is always there to protect us. Even if
we may not actually see Him with our physical eyes, we can
have confidence that He is ready to intervene.

God's Word provides plenty of direction in praying for protection. King David prayed, *"Keep me as the apple of your eye; hide me in the shadow of your wings."* (Psalm 17:8)

Solomon writes, *"My son, pay attention to what I say; turn your ear to my words. Do not let them out of your sight, keep them within your heart; for they are life to those who find them and health to one's whole body"* (Proverbs 4:20–22).

Jesus asks His Father to watch over and protect the disciples, but He also prays for *protection from Satan*. Jesus knows firsthand about spiritual warfare and that anyone serving God becomes a target. He also asks for a *full measure of joy* while they live in this world. Then, don't miss Jesus' request for their on-going *sanctification*. Sanctification is not an everyday word but a good one to know! It simply means to be made holy, to become like Christ who is holy. We too can ask the Father to use Scripture, music, nature, people or life experiences to open the eyes and heart of our loved ones so they may know Him better and become more like Him.

Interceding in prayer for others allows us to experience the joy of seeing God at work. He wants us to be constantly aware that *every good and perfect gift is from above, coming down from the Father of the heavenly lights, who does not change like shifting shadows* (James 1:17). The Creator of the Universe gives us the opportunity to join Him in His plan for another person. Committed disciples don't miss out!

Tomorrow we'll look at praying for God's plan for the Kingdom of God— the outer edges of our influence!

Jot It Down

- Search for other examples of prayers for protection. The Psalms are a rich source.

- Look for other passages that guide you in ways to pray for others.

Week Five, Day Three
Jesus Prays for All Believers

Jesus prayed, "*I pray not only for these, but also for those who believe in Me through their message*" (John 17:20, CSB). We are called by Jesus' example to go beyond our own needs and the needs of those in our inner circle. He wants us to pray for the needs of all believers—those throughout the world.

Jesus looked forward in time to those who would hear the Gospel through the disciples and would believe He was the Son of God. Now that's having God's vision for the world! Even then, I was on His mind. You were on His mind. Jesus envisioned believers from across the centuries. Can you see yourself in God's big picture? Will you be one of those disciples who will share the Truth with others?

Paul provides a helpful prayer model for us in Philippians 1:3–11. He shows such a tenderness toward the believers at the church in Philippi. As you read through this letter, look for *six things* we can pray for in the lives of those who we will one day meet in heaven.

> *3I thank my God every time I remember you. 4In all my prayers for all of you, I always pray with joy 5because of your partnership in the gospel from the first day until now, 6being confident of this, that he who began a good work in you will carry it on to completion until the day of Christ Jesus.*
>
> *7It is right for me to feel this way about all of you, since I have you in my heart and, whether I am in chains or defending and confirming the gospel, all of you share in God's grace with me. 8God can testify how I long for all of you with the affection of Christ Jesus.*

⁹And this is my prayer: that your love may abound more and more in knowledge and depth of insight, ¹⁰so that you may be able to discern what is best and may be pure and blameless for the day of Christ, ¹¹filled with the fruit of righteousness that comes through Jesus Christ—to the glory and praise of God (Phil. 1:3–11).

These are rich topics for discussion this week with your DM. I encourage you to pray together for all those who have not yet heard of God's love and for God to send someone to tell them. You might want to choose one of the six requests you identified above for your DM to pray for you.

Persecuted Believers

Daily we hear stories of persecuted believers. Some are denied the right to own a Bible. Others are forbidden to meet openly. Others are required to acknowledge allegiance to only their leaders instead of their Savior. They're imprisoned, sent to work camps, tortured or killed simply because they refuse to deny their faith in Jesus Christ. We must pray for these brothers and sisters in Christ that they will endure in their faith and be comforted by God's Holy Spirit. Refer back to the things Paul prayed for the Philippian believers

God has raised up many ways to keep us informed of how we can intercede for the missionaries and the believers they serve. Together with your DM, search out a resource you can use to guide your prayers for persecuted Christians. We all have much to learn as intercessors. No matter where we are in our understanding of prayer, we can always know God hears us anytime, anywhere and about anything He places on our hearts. Open your heart as Jesus did to the Father!

Week Five, Day Four
Jesus Prays for Unity

My husband flew as a career pilot. He loved everything about flying! Today, a wide variety of planes and pilots crowd the skies. In spite of the differences, each pilot must obey instructions from the tower when he's landing or taking off for harmony in the skies. That's how unity works in a Christian's life. We must follow the instructions from our Savior, particularly in relation to other believers, to experience this unity.

Jesus prayed, "*may they all be one, as You, Father, are in Me and I am in You. May they also be one in Us, so the world may believe You sent Me*" (John 17:21). Unity requires vulnerability. Have you ever been hurt by a fellow Christian? Maybe they spoke unkind words or shared one of your confidences. Even what might initially appear insignificant can create disunity. Relationships require trust, especially among believers in community. Even sharing prayer requests requires sensitivity and respect for others.

Jot it Down

- Reflect upon the last time you got caught in disunity or told others something confidentially entrusted to you. Remember the discord that resulted?
- Take time to ask God to forgive you and to give you the courage to resolve any hurt that might have resulted.
- Journal your thoughts and consider discussing this with your DM.

The apostle Paul instructs the believers in Philippi in how to develop unified and loving relationships. *If then there is any encouragement in Christ, if any consolation of love, if any fellowship with the Spirit, if any affection and mercy, fulfill my joy by thinking the same way, having the same love, sharing the same feelings, focusing on one goal.* (Philippians 1:1–2, CSB)

Notice the four "ifs" that Paul listed:

- If there is any encouragement in Christ
- If any consolation of love
- If any fellowship with the Spirit
- If any affection and mercy

Paul wanted them to share in his goal of having these same qualities of encouragement, consolation, fellowship, affection and mercy demonstrated among the believers in Philippi—which would have resulted in unity.

In the movie *Invictus*, I was impressed with Nelson Mandela's indomitable passion for creating unity within South Africa and his strategy of using rugby to accomplish his goal. Unity in government is desirable as much as unity within communities. Unity in the body of Christ, though, is essential. Perhaps the best portrayal of unity among believers is when denominations come together in an outreach or ministry. It's unity at work. In fact, it's so important that Jesus prayed to His Father asking for it for the disciples. Jesus even gave the reason why it's so important—*so the world may believe You sent Me.*

Disciples not only seek unity but work to preserve unity among believers. Discuss with your DM both positive and negative experiences you've had in relationships with other Christians.

Journaling Growth

- Key thoughts from the passage
- A commandment for me to obey or an example to follow
- How can I apply one of these truths to my life today?
- Prayer requests for myself, my family, others
- Things I want to discuss with my DM

The Disciple's Comfort
WEEK SIX

Overview

This week we focus on the way Jesus comforted his disciples. Here's the occasion. They had eaten together then shared the humbling experience of having Jesus wash their feet. Such intimate fellowship! That's when Jesus said, "One of you will betray me." After giving the piece of bread to the betrayer, Judas, Jesus added, "What you're doing do quickly." Judas immediately left. Peter then asked the first question.

> *"Lord," Simon Peter said to Him, "where are You going?"*
>
> *Jesus answered, "Where I am going you cannot follow Me now, but you will follow later"* (John 13:35, CSB).

The disciples had traveled with Jesus day and night for three years. Now, he spoke of leaving him. What loss! Why? Where was He going? What would they do without Jesus? This uncertainty provides the backdrop for this passage. As you read, ask God to open your heart and mind to the tender words of Jesus as he addresses their concerns.

> *"Do not let your hearts be troubled. You believe in God; believe also in me. ²My Father's house has many rooms; if that were not so, would I have told you that I am going there*

to prepare a place for you? **³**And if I go and prepare a place for you, I will come back and take you to be with me that you also may be where I am. **⁴**You know the way to the place where I am going."

⁵Thomas said to him, "Lord, we don't know where you are going, so how can we know the way?"

⁶Jesus answered, "I am the way and the truth and the life. No one comes to the Father except through me. **⁷**If you really know me, you will know my Father as well. From now on, you do know him and have seen him."

⁸Philip said, "Lord, show us the Father and that will be enough for us."

⁹Jesus answered: "Don't you know me, Philip, even after I have been among you such a long time? Anyone who has seen me has seen the Father. How can you say, 'Show us the Father'? **¹⁰**Don't you believe that I am in the Father, and that the Father is in me? The words I say to you I do not speak on my own authority. Rather, it is the Father, living in me, who is doing his work. **¹¹**Believe me when I say that I am in the Father and the Father is in me; or at least believe on the evidence of the works themselves" (John 14:1–11).

Simplified Outline

I. Jesus talks about heaven (verses 1–4)
    A. The Father's house has many places to live.
    B. Jesus is going to prepare a place for them.
    C. He will come back for the disciples.
II. Jesus talks about Himself (verses 5–11)
    A. He is the way, the truth and the life.
    B. No one comes to the Father except through Him.

    C. The one who has seen Jesus has seen the Father.

III. Jesus talks about prayer (verses 12–14)

    A. Believers will do even greater work.

    B. He will do whatever they ask in His name.

    C. This will bring glory to the Father.

IV. Jesus talks about the Holy Spirit (verses 15–25)

    A. He will ask the Father to send another Counselor.

    B. The Spirit of Truth will live within those who believe in Him.

    C. The Father will come to those who love Him.

    D. The Holy Spirit will teach them and remind them of what they have been taught.

V. Jesus talks about peace (verses 26–27)

    A. He will leave peace with them.

    B. His peace will be different from the world's.

    C. Do not be troubled or afraid.

Week Six, Day One
Jesus Provides for All Our Needs

When Jesus said, "Do not let your hearts be troubled," He wasn't referring to sadness but to their confusion and anxiety about all He was saying. These words are far more than a friend saying, "Don't worry. It's going to be ok." Jesus' admonition is based on God's character and His Word. Today, when we apply Jesus's words to our lives, it's based upon His provision for us. Jesus cares about every need in our lives. He will provide for each one (Phil. 4:19).

Jesus further challenged the disciples to believe in Him, to trust Him. "*Believe in God; believe also in Me.*" It's amazing to think that after all this time, the disciples still struggled with trusting Jesus as God Himself. It's easy to let your circumstances overshadow how immense God truly is. When I have an unexpected financial need, I paraphrase Psalm 50:10, "*My God owns the cattle on a thousand hills.*" That has specific meaning because I live in the country and know the value of cattle! Ask the Lord to give you a verse/promise to hang on to the next time you need comforting.

Jesus next shares a promise of another source of comfort. "*In My Father's house are many dwelling places; if not, I would have told you. I am going away to prepare a place for you. If I go away and prepare a place for you, I will come back and receive you to Myself, so that where I am you may be also*" (John 14:2, 3, CSB). Can't you hear His love for these men and how He longs for the day they will be together forever?

Why do you think Jesus picked this time to tell them about what He'd be doing when He left them? Perhaps He knew it would provide comfort knowing He had a plan in place for their future together. It certainly comforts me knowing I too will one day be together with my Christian family and friends who have died. It overcomes those fears of the finality of death.

Tomorrow we will look at the promise of the Holy Spirit. Spend some time thanking the Father for all the ways He has provided for you.

Jot It Down

- What troubles you? Writing it down will help clarify your anxious thoughts. If you talk to Jesus about it, you'll be able to say, "I've given this concern to Jesus and I can trust Him to take care of it." Now, trust Him to do just that!

Week Six, Day Two
The Promise of the Holy Spirit

"Very truly I tell you, whoever believes in me will do the works I have been doing, and they will do even greater things than these, because I am going to the Father. [13]And I will do what-

> ever you ask in my name, so that the Father may be glorified
> in the Son. **14** You may ask me for anything in my name, and
> I will do it.
>
> **15** "If you love me, keep my commands. **16** And I will ask the
> Father, and he will give you another advocate to help you and
> be with you forever—**17** the Spirit of truth. The world cannot
> accept him, because it neither sees him nor knows him. But
> you know him, for he lives with you and will be] in you. **18** I will
> not leave you as orphans; I will come to you" (John 14:12–18).

Based upon this passage, a believer can know they are a Christian because they have the Holy Spirit within them. That's something to truly celebrate! If the Holy Spirit lives within you, then you will also be able to learn how to identify that still small voice within you speaking truth to your heart and mind.

> "If you love Me you will keep My commandments. And I will
> ask the Father, and He will give you another Counselor to be
> with you forever. He is the Spirit of truth. The world is unable
> to receive Him because it doesn't see Him or know Him. But
> you do know Him, because He remains with you and will be
> in you. I will not leave you as orphans; I am coming to you"
> (John 14:15–18, CSB).

The Holy Spirit is part of the Trinity: Father, Son and Holy Spirit. Jesus asked the Father to send the Holy Spirit to believers so they wouldn't feel like orphans. More comforting words! Nonbelievers do not see nor know the Spirit. This awareness helps explain some of their choices. It also explains the behaviors of Christians who do not choose to draw upon this amazing power within them.

"I have spoken these things to you while I remain with you. But the Counselor, the Holy Spirit—the Father will send Him in My name—will teach you all things and remind you of everything I have told you" (John 14:25, 26, CSB).

Here the Holy Spirit is called the *Paraclete.* It means "a person called to the side in order to help." The disciples understood the word and it's meaning in a deeper way than we initially grasp. How comforting! Jesus also instructed the disciples that the Spirit would teach and remind them of everything He had taught them. Another reassuring thought.

Perhaps you've discovered additional work of the Spirit. He guides us into truth, helps brings glory to Jesus, as well as convicts the world of sin and the need for righteousness. These are the things that drew each of us to know Jesus' salvation—because of the work of the Holy Spirit. I had a personal experience that impacted me in understanding the presence and protection of the Holy Spirit in my life.

Shirley's Snippets

I was enjoying a relaxing time of worshiping and walking on the country road near my home when I heard loud, angry barking. Two terrifying Doberman dogs paced and growled just ahead. Fortunately, a chain link fence stood between them and me. Even so, I crossed to the other side of the road before resuming my singing. I reached my three-mile mark and turned to head home when I realized those vicious dogs stood six feet in front of me. I froze. I then heard in my spirit, "Just keep walking and listen to Me. Do not stop or look at them." As I passed by, they stood perfectly still and silent. The Holy Spirit protected me by providing instruction and courage to move forward. I learned that very day a lifelong lesson of focusing on God rather than on my fear.

Jesus told His disciples, "*I will not leave you as orphans; I am coming to you.*" This promise is true for us too. He will guide us as well. Jesus will not leave any believer without the Helper, the Spirit. He lives within us as an invaluable resource, anytime we look to Him for protection, guidance, wisdom or courage!

Jot It Down

- Identify a terrifying time when God protected you.
- Like many others, do you also struggle with anxiety?
- Search for scriptures that can be a source of comfort.

Week Six, Day Three
Promise of Fellowship

"I will not leave you as orphans; I will come to you. ¹⁹Before long, the world will not see me anymore, but you will see me. Because I live, you also will live. ²⁰On that day you will realize that I am in my Father, and you are in me, and I am in you. ²¹Whoever has my commands and keeps them is the one who loves me. The one who loves me will be loved by my Father, and I too will love them and show myself to them."

²²Then Judas (not Judas Iscariot) said, "But, Lord, why do you intend to show yourself to us and not to the world?"

²³Jesus replied, "Anyone who loves me will obey my teaching. My Father will love them, and we will come to them and make our home with them. ²⁴Anyone who does not love me will not obey my teaching. These words you hear are not my own; they belong to the Father who sent me."

⁵"All this I have spoken while still with you. ²⁶But the Advocate, the Holy Spirit, whom the Father will send in my name, will teach you all things and will remind you of everything I have said to you" (John 14:18–26).

Shirley's Snippets

We are created for community. I treasure childhood holidays visiting my grandmother. The men usually talked outside while the women and children gathered in the living room. I enjoyed hearing my mother's, aunts' and grandmother's humorous stories until—as my mother would say—I got to acting up. Mother quickly sent me to a separate room to "be alone with my thoughts."

Today we read how Jesus will be leaving His own disciples alone with their thoughts when He returns to heaven. In their three years with Jesus, they could interact face-to-face with their Teacher. In John 14, Jesus explained they would no longer be together physically for the fellowship they had enjoyed.

"Before long, the world will not see me anymore, but you will see me. Because I live, you also will live. ²⁰On that day you will realize that I am in my Father, and you are in me, and I am in you. ²¹Whoever has my commands and keeps them is the one who loves me. The one who loves me will be loved by my Father, and I too will love them and show myself to them."

²²Then Judas (not Judas Iscariot) said, "But, Lord, why do you intend to show yourself to us and not to the world?"

²³Jesus replied, "Anyone who loves me will obey my teaching. My Father will love them, and we will come to them and make our home with them. ²⁴Anyone who does not love me will not obey my teaching. These words you hear are not my own; they belong to the Father who sent me" (John 14:19–24).

Powerful summary statements of this passage:

- The world will no longer see Jesus.
- The disciples would see Jesus.
- The Father and Jesus will come and make their home with those who love them.
- The phrase *the one who loves Jesus* indicates it's an individual choice for each of us.

An explanation for the phrase *in that day* is found in Acts 2:1, 2, 14.

> *When the day of Pentecost came, they were all together in one place.* *²Suddenly a sound like the blowing of a violent wind came from heaven and filled the whole house where they were sitting….* *¹⁴Then Peter stood up with the Eleven, raised his voice and addressed the crowd: "Fellow Jews and all of you who live in Jerusalem, let me explain this to you; listen carefully to what I say."*

In Acts, the promised gift of the Holy Spirit's indwelling arrived on earth sent from the Father. The Father, Son and Holy Spirit are now available to all believers. The prophet Zephaniah prophesized what those days would be like for those who lived a repentant and faithful life.

> *Sing, Daughter Zion;*
> *shout aloud, Israel!*
> *Be glad and rejoice with all your heart,*
> *Daughter Jerusalem!*
> *¹⁵The LORD has taken away your punishment,*
> *he has turned back your enemy.*
> *The LORD, the King of Israel, is with you;*
> *never again will you fear any harm.*

16On that day

they will say to Jerusalem,

"Do not fear, Zion;

do not let your hands hang limp.

17The LORD your God is with you,

the Mighty Warrior who saves.

He will take great delight in you;

in his love he will no longer rebuke you,

but will rejoice over you with singing"

(Zephaniah 3:14–17).

Zephaniah foretold what this type of repentant fellowship with God would feel like. God rejoices over us with gladness; He quiets us in love, and He rejoices over us with singing. We belong to God. He redeemed us through Christ and placed His Spirit in us so that we can experience close fellowship with Him. We will never lose our relationship with the Father, Son and the Holy Spirit, but we could face broken fellowship with Him if we choose our own path instead of His. We show our love for Jesus through obedience providing proof that we are His disciples. A disciple must follow Jesus' commands as well in order to experience this close fellowship.

Jot It Down

- Those who didn't grow up in a loving home may have a distorted concept of nurturing families. John 14:23 describes the best kind of family possible. *Jesus answered, "If anyone loves Me, he will keep My word. My Father will love him, and We will come to him and make Our home with him."* Realize that you belong to the family of God. Christ wants to make your heart His home.

- Describe the kind of home you grew up in and discuss it with your DM or small group leader.
- Record any reflections you have from the summary statements of John 14:19–24 and the phrase *in that day.*

Week Six, Day Four
The Peace of Jesus

We've examined how to find comfort in knowing that God will supply our needs. We now know He has given us a Helper so we will never be alone. We've also learned how we can have fellowship with the Creator of the universe. Now we direct our attention to the peace Jesus gives us, true peace. "*Peace I leave with you. My peace I give to you. I do not give to you as the world gives. Your heart must not be troubled or fearful*" (John 14:27 CSB).

Jesus could have left his disciples many things—wealth, fame or prestige. But He knew exactly what these men whom he loved so much would need in order to share the gospel. They would face many hardships. In the end, all but John would die a martyr's death sharing these truths. Jesus knew they would need His constant peace.

This is the same peace that Paul spoke of in Philippians 4:6-7, "*Do not be anxious about anything, but in every situation, by prayer and petition, with thanksgiving, present your requests to God.*"

Paul tells us:

- Don't worry about anything.
- Share our requests to God through prayer and petition.
- These actions allow us to experience God's peace.
- This peace will guard our hearts and minds.

The world offers you many things—outward pleasures, wealth, beauty and honor; but it can never provide the inner peace that comes from knowing Jesus. When this peace enters our heart, it begins driving away fear and anxiety. It will help you face the unknown future. Even when you're not aware of His peace, it will be available when you draw upon it.

As I think about John 14, Jesus appears to be speaking as if He knew the sorrow that was in their hearts. He's gentle and takes His time with them even when He was interrupted by their questions. He wanted to let them know they were loved.

Shirley's Snippets

In the early years of marriage, my husband interviewed for a pilot's job in California. We lived in Texas, and I had family and responsibilities that kept me in the Lone Star State. My heart ached. I had no idea when I would see him again. He was to fly for one month on a trial basis. On the day we left to catch his flight, I drove as slowly as possible. Even though my despair felt very real to me, I imagine it was just a glimpse of what the disciples felt as they faced Jesus' departure.

Jot It Down

- List times when you felt comfort from God. Perhaps it was a verse, a song, or words of a friend.
- Spend a few minutes in prayer thanking God that you can always trust Him to bring you comfort when you need it the most.

Journaling Growth

- List key thoughts of the passage
- Commandments I should obey or an example to follow

- Application
- Prayer requests for my family, myself or others
- Things to discuss with my DM

The Disciple's Fruit
WEEK SEVEN

Overview

We've discussed characteristics of a disciple willing to offer "all of me" to Christ. Today we'll discover how God produces these qualities in a believer's life. I learned about the source of our strength early in my Christian journey when I was asked to share my testimony with a group of women. I felt such terror that I couldn't even get out of my car in the parking lot. I sat there crying and praying. Then, I remembered John 15:8, *My Father is glorified by this; that you produce much fruit and prove to be my disciples.* God sent the courage I needed to get out of the car. I planted this verse in my heart as a reminder of my desire to bring my Father glory by bearing much fruit. I desire for this week's passage to also speak to your heart. We'll learn that one of the defining marks of a disciple of Jesus is fruit resulting from a growing relationship with Him.

> *"I am the true vine, and my Father is the gardener. ²He cuts off every branch in me that bears no fruit, while every branch that does bear fruit he prunes so that it will be even more fruitful. ³You are already clean because of the word I have spoken to you. ⁴Remain in me, as I also remain in you. No*

branch can bear fruit by itself; it must remain in the vine. Neither can you bear fruit unless you remain in me.

⁵"I am the vine; you are the branches. If you remain in me and I in you, you will bear much fruit; apart from me you can do nothing. ⁶If you do not remain in me, you are like a branch that is thrown away and withers; such branches are picked up, thrown into the fire and burned.⁷If you remain in me and my words remain in you, ask whatever you wish, and it will be done for you. ⁸This is to my Father's glory, that you bear much fruit, showing yourselves to be my disciples" (John 15:1–8).

Simplified Outline

I.   The vine and the branches (verse 1)
   A. Jesus is the vine
   B. The Father is the gardener
II. The Father is the vine keeper (verses 2-4)
   A. Removes branches that don't produce fruit
   B. Prunes branches that do
   C. Throws aside those not remaining in Christ
III. The disciples are the branches (verses 5-8)
   A. Can't produce fruit without the vine
   B. Must remain in Jesus
   C. Glorify the Father when they produce fruit
   D. Ask what they want
   E. Prove they are disciples by their fruit

Week Seven, Day One
The True Vine

I can imagine Jesus and His disciples walking and talking when Jesus breaks off a branch from a grapevine and begins to teach them about their relationship in the days ahead. Calvary and the cross loomed before Him, but for now, He focused on equipping his followers for His departure.

> *"I am the true vine, and my Father is the gardener. ²He cuts off every branch in me that bears no fruit, while every branch that does bear fruit he prunes so that it will be even more fruitful. ³You are already clean because of the word I have spoken to you. ⁴Remain in me, as I also remain in you. No branch can bear fruit by itself; it must remain in the vine. Neither can you bear fruit unless you remain in me.*
>
> *⁵"I am the vine; you are the branches. If you remain in me and I in you, you will bear much fruit; apart from me you can do nothing. ⁶If you do not remain in me, you are like a branch that is thrown away and withers; such branches are picked up, thrown into the fire and burned. ⁷If you remain in me and my words remain in you, ask whatever you wish, and it will be done for you. ⁸This is to my Father's glory, that you bear much fruit, showing yourselves to be my disciples"* (John 15:1–8).

Jesus taught in verse one, "*I am the true vine.*" As Jews, the disciples would most likely have associated Jesus' announcement with the numerous Old Testament writings that portrayed Israel as a vine. He's the *real* vine, contrasted with the failure of the vine of Israel to fulfill it's calling to produce fruit for God. He wanted the disciples to know the truth about who He was in this parable and not be confused by the analogy. To help His disciples remain faithful, He explained what they needed to know about how they would serve Him in the future.

> *"I am the true vine, and my Father is the gardener. ²He cuts off every branch in me that bears no fruit, while every branch*

that does bear fruit he prunes so that it will be even more fruitful."

- Fruit bearing begins with a vine and a vine dresser.
- The vine provides the source of nourishment.
- Branches must remain in the vine to produce fruit.
- Dead branches that don't produce fruit are tossed aside.
- Branches that do produce fruit are pruned.

The key phrase in verse two is "in Me." This lets us know where our focus should be—remaining and drawing our strength and nourishment from the vine. The Father is the keeper of the vineyard. He is the one who does the pruning that results in more fruit. The pruning process is often painful and difficult, but the Father deeply loves those He prunes.

Luke 22:31, 32 provides an example of Peter in a pruning process:

> *"Simon, Simon, Satan has asked to sift all of you as wheat. ³²But I have prayed for you, Simon, that your faith may not fail. And when you have turned back, strengthen your brothers."*

Notice that Jesus prayed for Peter and told him to strengthen his brothers when he turned back to his faith. It will not be easy to remain faithful to Jesus. You'll be tempted to compromise, walk away or give in to sin. Do not retreat. Stay in the battle. We have a Father who is greater than all of your struggles. He is the source of our strength and will fight for us.

Jot It Down

- Describe a current pruning experience or one from the past.
- What have you learned from these times? Be encouraged about this process. Jesus lovingly acts on our behalf when we go through this process.

Week Seven, Day Two
The True Relationship

Have you ever been concerned about not having evidence of God at work in your life? I know I have. Look Jesus' words in John 15:3-4.

> *You are already clean because of the word I have spoken to you. Remain in Me, and I in you. Just as a branch is unable to produce fruit by itself unless it remains on the vine, so neither can you unless you remain in Me.*

The qualification for bearing fruit is remaining in Jesus. Stay connected to the vine! What does this look like? What must I do?

1. **Remaining in Jesus begins with staying in close fellowship with Him.**

How are you currently doing this? I have found if I'm diligent about my personal devotions in the study of God's Word, prayer and confession of my sins, my relationship with God increases in intimacy. That's how I've been able to receive direction and reassurance from God. You will too.

2. **Remaining in Jesus requires that you be available to Him.**

Offering yourself to Him with your time and attention is part of abiding. It also includes spending time reading God's Word and in prayer. If we don't remain in Christ, we'll lead barren, fruitless lives. But if we do remain, we'll reap the rewards. We will bear fruit! It's the outcome of being available and being obedient.

Jot It Down

- Think through the things that you struggle with and that keep you from being available to Jesus.
- What is your plan for being accessible to the True Vine?

- If you have trouble spending daily quality time with Jesus, discuss it with your DM or small group leader.
- Andrew Murray wrote in *Abide in Christ*, "The safety and fruitfulness of the branch depends upon the strength of the vine." How strong do you believe Jesus is? What difference does that make in your discipleship journey?
- Record the ways Jesus has revealed His strength in the Scriptures we've studied together.

3. **Remaining in Jesus means depending on the Vine.**

Verse 4 says, "*Just as a branch is unable to produce fruit by itself unless it remains on the vine, so neither can you unless you remain in Me.*" We must be totally dependent on the vine. This involves submitting ourselves completely to Him, offering our "all." Many times, I've held on to things I wanted to control. How about you? Are you holding onto something? A secret white lie? A judgmental attitude? Bitterness toward someone? Give it up today! Any area you do not give over to Him will keep you from depending on the vine.

Jot It Down

- Record things you hold onto, things you want to control. Stop and ask His forgiveness.
- John 15:9, 10, offers additional guidance on how to remain in the vine. "*As the Father has loved Me, I have also loved you. Remain in My love. If you keep My commands you will remain in My love, just as I have kept My Father's commands and remain in His love*" (CSB). What is the key to remaining in the vine?

4. **Remaining in Jesus includes loving Him.**

Our love for Jesus can be hard to express at times. It might be through praise and worship, thankfulness or even drawing near to Him for comfort. It's exhibited in our joy from reading God's Word and the

Holy Spirit communicating truth to us. It can also be expressed through loving and caring for others.

Jesus' love for His disciples was so great that He compared it to His Father's love for Himself. I don't really know how to measure this kind of Love, but Jesus provides direction for experiencing it.

5. **Remaining in Jesus includes keeping His commandments.**
John 15:10 gives the results of the rebirth we talked about earlier. Changes may be small and gradual, but they should be evident. As we grow in Christ, our life begins to change as we learn obedience from abiding. One thing you'll begin to notice is a growing love for others. 1 John 4:16 says, "*And so we know and rely on the love God has for us. God is love. Whoever lives in love lives in God, and God in them.*"

If we are to bear fruit, then we must stay in close fellowship with Christ, make ourselves available to Him, depend on Him alone and love Jesus by keeping His commandments without compromise. Tomorrow we'll study the nature of the fruit we produce as His branches.

Week Seven, Day Three
The Nature of the Fruit

When I first became a Christian, I was more concerned about my spiritual gift and less concerned about the fruit my life produced for God's glory. That was a huge mistake!

Spiritual fruit is distinct from spiritual gifts. Paul addresses spiritual gifts in Romans 12:4–5 and 1 Cor. 12:4–11.

> "*I am the true vine, and my Father is the gardener. ²He cuts off every branch in me that bears no fruit, while every branch that does bear fruit he prunes[a] so that it will be even more fruitful. ³You are already clean because of the word I have*

79

spoken to you. ⁴Remain in me, as I also remain in you. No branch can bear fruit by itself; it must remain in the vine. Neither can you bear fruit unless you remain in me.

⁵"I am the vine; you are the branches. If you remain in me and I in you, you will bear much fruit; apart from me you can do nothing. ⁶If you do not remain in me, you are like a branch that is thrown away and withers; such branches are picked up, thrown into the fire and burned. ⁷If you remain in me and my words remain in you, ask whatever you wish, and it will be done for you. ⁸This is to my Father's glory, that you bear much fruit, showing yourselves to be my disciples" (John 15:1–8).

Notice the progression in how much fruit is produced by a branch in John 15:

- Verse two mentions branches that bear "no" fruit.
- Verse two then mentions pruning branches that do bear "some" fruit to produce "more" fruit.
- Verse eight references bearing "much" fruit.
- None—some—more—much

Evidences of spiritual fruit can be found on the inside and outside areas of our life if you remain in the vine. I've shared an example below of a time when I first noticed God was beginning to produce fruit in my life. These earliest evidences of God working truly imprint our minds and encourage us forward. I'm so thankful for Jesus' great love and patience with us!

Shirley's Snippets

I had been a follower of Christ about a year and wondered if God had produced any fruit in my life so I asked Him to show me if I was growing. While volunteering at a wedding at our church, God gave me a glimpse into His work in my heart. The bride suddenly appeared and abruptly directed me to "follow her." I quietly and quickly trailed her to solve the problem at hand. In my spirit, I heard the Lord say to me, "See, you *have* changed." It was true. Before Christ was in my life, I would have replied with a quick retort about the tone of her voice. I *had* changed, and I could see the fruit of my loving reaction. I can remember not how my heart overflowed with gratefulness to God.

The Nature of Believers' Fruit

The following verses explain the nature of the fruit believers produce. Pick out the descriptions and discuss them with your DM or small group.

But the fruit of the Spirit is love, joy, peace, forbearance, kindness, good-ness, faithfulness, gentleness and self-control (Gal. 5:22, 23).

Produce fruit in keeping with repentance.... Every tree that does not produce good fruit will be cut down and thrown into the fire (Matt. 3:8, 10).

By their fruit you will recognize them. Do people pick grapes from thorn-bushes? Likewise, every good tree bears good fruit, but a bad tree bears bad fruit. A good tree cannot bear bad fruit, and a bad tree cannot bear good fruit. Every tree that does not bear good fruit is cut down and thrown into the fire. Thus, by their fruit you will recognize them (Matt. 7:16–20).

(Paul writes) I do not want you to be unaware, brothers and sisters, that I planned many times to come to you...in order that I might have a harvest

among you, just as I have had among the other Gentiles (Romans 1:13–17).

...the gospel is bearing fruit and growing throughout the whole world—just as it has been doing among you since the day you heard it and truly understood God's grace (Col. 1:6).

Peacemakers who sow in peace reap a harvest of righteousness (James 3:18).

Your good fruit may exhibit itself in your optimistic attitude, kind gestures, pure words, thoughtful deeds or changed motives. Each time you notice good fruit in your life, thank Jesus for showing you how to remain in the vine!

Week Seven, Day Four
Failure to Connect

Today's discussion is painful to consider but vital to address: some do not connect with Jesus as their Lord and Savior even though they have the opportunity. Judas, the one who betrayed Jesus, is a good example.

> *"If anyone does not remain in Me, he is thrown aside like a branch and he withers. They gather them, throw them into the fire, and they are burned"* (John 15:6).

Jesus spoke of individuals who heard of God's love shown in Jesus Christ, lingered to listen, then chose to walk away. Such tragedy! Like dead branches on a vine, they are tossed away, they wither and are burned. If you know someone who is faltering in committing to Christ, stop and pray that their eyes and heart might be opened to the Truth of who Christ is.

Joyful News

Joyfully, verses 7 and 8 of John 15 contain an amazing promise for abiding believers.

> *"If you remain in Me and My words remain in you ask whatever you want and it will be done for you. My Father is glorified by this: that you produce much fruit and **prove*** (emphasis mine) *to be My disciples"* (John 15:7-8).

One change I've noticed in my life relates to my prayer life. It's grown from reciting a list of requests to asking what God desires of me. I want to be a fruit-producing member of the body of Christ. I'm discovering that I'm asking forgiveness for sinful attitudes and other heart issues. The more the Holy Spirit aligns our lives with His Word, the more our hearts reflect God's heart. As a result, our prayers will be in accordance with the Father's will—and fruit appears through our prayers!

Jot It Down

- Consider whether you're drawing your strength from God in such a way that He is able to produce His fruit in your life. Explain.
- What words would you use to describe your current connection with Christ?
- Many religions require their followers to earn a spot in heaven. Devoted followers of Christ desire to glorify their crucified and risen Savior by the way they live their lives in response to His great love. Record your thoughts about your personal motivation for living for Christ. Is it motivated by rituals or a response to His love?

Journaling Growth

- Key thoughts from John 15:1–8

- Is there a commandment I should obey or an example to follow?
- How can I apply these truths to my life today?
- Prayer requests for my family, myself or others
- Things I need to discuss with my DM

The Disciple's Commitment—All of Me
WEEK EIGHT

Overview

My prayer has been that this journey has brought you closer to the Father and has encouraged you to be a fruit-bearing disciple as you learn how to offer Him "all of me." This week we'll examine an additional characteristic of a fruitful follower of Jesus—sharing the gospel story with others.

One year my husband surprised me with a garden fountain depicting the woman at the well, the one often referred to as the Samaritan woman in John 4. I enjoy sitting on my porch as water pours from her jar and think about the conversation she had with Jesus. What began as a simple request for a drink ended up in personal salvation for her and others in the village. I hope this week will encourage you to have a heart for those you meet who do not have a saving relationship with Jesus. Our passage is in John 4:1–42. It's the longest passage we've worked through, but I'm confident you'll find the story intriguing!

Now Jesus learned that the Pharisees had heard that he was gaining and baptizing more disciples than John—²although in fact it was not Jesus who baptized, but his disciples. ³*So he left Judea and went back once more to Galilee.*

⁴*Now he had to go through Samaria.* ⁵*So he came to a town in Samaria called Sychar, near the plot of ground Jacob had given to his son Joseph.* ⁶*Jacob's well was there, and Jesus, tired as he was from the journey, sat down by the well. It was about noon.*

⁷*When a Samaritan woman came to draw water, Jesus said to her, "Will you give me a drink?"* ⁸*(His disciples had gone into the town to buy food.)*

⁹*The Samaritan woman said to him, "You are a Jew and I am a Samaritan woman. How can you ask me for a drink?" (For Jews do not associate with Samaritans.)*

¹⁰*Jesus answered her, "If you knew the gift of God and who it is that asks you for a drink, you would have asked him and he would have given you living water."*

¹¹*"Sir," the woman said, "you have nothing to draw with and the well is deep. Where can you get this living water?* ¹²*Are you greater than our father Jacob, who gave us the well and drank from it himself, as did also his sons and his livestock?"*

¹³*Jesus answered, "Everyone who drinks this water will be thirsty again,* ¹⁴ *but whoever drinks the water I give them will never thirst. Indeed, the water I give them will become in them a spring of water welling up to eternal life."*

¹⁵*The woman said to him, "Sir, give me this water so that I won't get thirsty and have to keep coming here to draw water."*

¹⁶*He told her, "Go, call your husband and come back."*

¹⁷*"I have no husband," she replied.*

Jesus said to her, "You are right when you say you have no husband. **18**The fact is, you have had five husbands, and the man you now have is not your husband. What you have just said is quite true."

19"Sir," the woman said, "I can see that you are a prophet. **20**Our ancestors worshiped on this mountain, but you Jews claim that the place where we must worship is in Jerusalem."

21"Woman," Jesus replied, "believe me, a time is coming when you will worship the Father neither on this mountain nor in Jerusalem. **22**You Samaritans worship what you do not know; we worship what we do know, for salvation is from the Jews. **23**Yet a time is coming and has now come when the true worshipers will worship the Father in the Spirit and in truth, for they are the kind of worshipers the Father seeks. **24**God is spirit, and his worshipers must worship in the Spirit and in truth."

25The woman said, "I know that Messiah" (called Christ) "is coming. When he comes, he will explain everything to us."

26Then Jesus declared, "I, the one speaking to you—I am he."

27Just then his disciples returned and were surprised to find him talking with a woman. But no one asked, "What do you want?" or "Why are you talking with her?"

28Then, leaving her water jar, the woman went back to the town and said to the people, **29**"Come, see a man who told me everything I ever did. Could this be the Messiah?" **30**They came out of the town and made their way toward him.

31Meanwhile his disciples urged him, "Rabbi, eat something."

32But he said to them, "I have food to eat that you know nothing about."

33Then his disciples said to each other, "Could someone have brought him food?"

34"My food," said Jesus, "is to do the will of him who sent me and to finish his work. 35Don't you have a saying, 'It's still four months until harvest'? I tell you, open your eyes and look at the fields! They are ripe for harvest. 36Even now the one who reaps draws a wage and harvests a crop for eternal life, so that the sower and the reaper may be glad together. 37Thus the saying 'One sows and another reaps' is true. 38I sent you to reap what you have not worked for. Others have done the hard work, and you have reaped the benefits of their labor."

39Many of the Samaritans from that town believed in him because of the woman's testimony, "He told me everything I ever did." 40So when the Samaritans came to him, they urged him to stay with them, and he stayed two days. 41And because of his words many more became believers.

42They said to the woman, "We no longer believe just because of what you said; now we have heard for ourselves, and we know that this man really is the Savior of the world."

Simplified Outline

I. Jesus heads to Galilee. (verses 1–4)
    A. His disciples had been baptizing.
    B. He left Judea.
    C. He traveled through Samaria.
II. Jesus talks about water and thirst. (verses 7–15)
    A. Jesus asks a woman for a drink.
    B. Jesus offers living water.
    C. The woman asks for the living water.
III. Jesus and the woman talk about her husband. (verses 16–19)

A. Jesus knows about her five husbands.

B. Jesus says the man she lives with is not her husband.

C. She believes Jesus is a prophet.

IV. Jesus and the woman talk about worship. (verses 20–26)

A. Salvation comes from the Jews.

B. God is spirit and we must worship in spirit and in truth.

C. Jesus identifies Himself as the Messiah.

V. The woman goes back into town. (verses 27–30)

A. Jesus' food is to do the will of the Father.

B. The fields are ready for harvest.

C. The sower and reaper can rejoice together.

VI. Jesus and the disciples talk about food. (verses 31–38).

A. Jesus' food is to do the will of the Father.

B. The fields are ready for harvest.

C. The sower and reaper can rejoice together.

VII. Samaritan villagers believe in Jesus (verses 39–42).

A. Jesus stayed two days.

B. Many believed because of what He said.

C. They believed Jesus was the Savior of the world.

Week Eight, Day One
A Conversation by a Well

This week we listen in on a private conversation between Jesus and a woman He met at a well. On His way to Galilee, Jesus stopped to rest at this historic spot in Samaria, Jacob's well. This sets the stage for fulfilling yet another ministry opportunity, or assignment, from His Father. I rejoice when I realize God has gone before me in orchestrating ministry moments. I desire that you develop that same anticipation. Being available to tell another person about Jesus demonstrates you have given your "all of me" to Jesus and bearing fruit that demonstrates (proves) you are a disciple of Christ.

The conversation began with a simple request in John 4. "Will you give me a drink?"

She replied, "*You are a Jew and I am a Samaritan woman. How can you ask me for a drink?*"

Jesus answered, "*If you knew the gift of God and who it is that asks you for a drink, you would have asked him and he would have given you living water.*"

As we speak with an unbeliever, we too must respond to any challenging response with gentleness. Also avoid religious terms that might create confusion and imply faith in Christ is complicated. Instead, keep the conversation focused on Jesus. Their opportunity to hear about God's love through His Son's gift of salvation is priority.

Shirley's Snippets

I remember hearing Willie Robertson, the CEO of Duck Commander, tell about an experience in sharing his faith. While a guest in the home of a wealthy gentleman, he was asked what made his life different from so many other Christians'. What was the source of his hope? Because Willie knew how to share his faith, he was able to lead the man to Christ. Willie challenged his Christian audience to always be prepared with their testimony and the good news of Jesus Christ.

Peter also exhorted believers to have a ready answer in 1 Peter 3:15. "*Always be prepared to give an answer to everyone who asks you to give the reason for the hope that you have. But do this with gentleness and respect.*"

Connecting the Spiritual with Common

In this conversation at the well, Jesus began the conversation with common topics then made connections between spiritual truths and the physical world. Trust the Lord to guide you in seeing these connections when speaking to others about Him.

> *Jesus answered, "Everyone who drinks this water will be thirsty again, but whoever drinks the water I give them will never thirst. Indeed, the water I give them will become in them a spring of water welling up to eternal life."*

The woman said to him, "Sir, give me this water so that I won't get thirsty and have to keep coming here to draw water" (John 14:13–15).

Jot It Down

- We began this journey examining what it meant to believe in Jesus and to belong to Him. One way to summarize your personal testimony is to break it down into three parts. Use the categories below to discuss your story with your DM.

    1. What my life was like before I knew Jesus
    2. How I became a Christian
    3. What my life is like now that I know Jesus

- Record some typical responses of people in your community when asked about their spiritual journey. Perhaps include the excuses you had before becoming a follower of Christ. Here are some examples:
    "I used to go to church as a child but I don't go anymore."
    "People in church are just a bunch of hypocrites."
    "Many paths lead to God."

- Discuss any mental roadblocks you might have for sharing your faith with your DM.

Week Eight, Day Two
True Identity

We'll continue to eavesdrop on the conversation between Jesus and the woman at Jacob's well. Notice in verses John 4:19-20, how the woman redirects the conversation.

> Jesus answered, "Everyone who drinks this water will be thirsty again, [14]but whoever drinks the water I give them will never thirst. Indeed, the water I give them will become in them a spring of water welling up to eternal life."
>
> [15]The woman said to him, "Sir, give me this water so that I won't get thirsty and have to keep coming here to draw water."
>
> [16]He told her, "Go, call your husband and come back."
>
> [17]"I have no husband," she replied.
>
> Jesus said to her, "You are right when you say you have no husband. [18]The fact is, you have had five husbands, and the man you now have is not your husband. What you have just said is quite true."
>
> [19]"Sir," the woman said, "I can see that you are a prophet."

Consider how an unbeliever might feel when we first begin to talk about Jesus. Gentleness and patience will help open doors. Approach others with a humble spirit and pray your words will be used by the Holy Spirit to begin His work in their lives. As the Holy Spirit develops a genuine caring in our hearts, we'll feel freer to offer our time and attention for a relaxed, comfortable conversation.

Don't compare yourself with trained teachers of God's Word. It's not eloquence but the Spirit of God that impacts lives. Be encouraged! Through yielding to the Spirit's leading, you too can be effective in sharing truth with an unbeliever. Just make yourself available!

Notice how Jesus directed the conversation from physical water to living water, helping her see her true need, the same need we all have—the need for a Savior, the source of living water. Jesus told her to call her husband to bring the conversation back to heart issues—the need for a Savior. God used Jesus' knowledge of her life to bring her to awareness that Jesus surely must be a prophet! We don't know how long the conversation continued, but she obviously wanted to hear more from Jesus and to remain in His presence.

Jot It Down

- Reflect upon a time you lingered to listen to God's truth? Was it a conversation, a podcast, a devotional time or a sermon? What were you learning? What do you remember?

The conversation continues in verses 20–26.

> *20Our ancestors worshiped on this mountain, but you Jews claim that the place where we must worship is in Jerusalem."*
>
> *21"Woman," Jesus replied, "believe me, a time is coming when you will worship the Father neither on this mountain nor in Jerusalem. 22You Samaritans worship what you do not know; we worship what we do know, for salvation is from the Jews. 23Yet a time is coming and has now come when the true worshipers will worship the Father in the Spirit and in truth, for they are the kind of worshipers the Father seeks. 24God is spirit, and his worshipers must worship in the Spirit and in truth."*

> *25The woman said, "I know that Messiah" (called Christ) "is coming. When he comes, he will explain everything to us."*
>
> *26Then Jesus declared, "I, the one speaking to you—I am he."*

Jesus identified Himself as the very One they'd been expecting. She actually stood in the presence of her Messiah! We too are blessed to know the Savior of the world and should never lose the wonder of that.

Stop for a moment and tell the Lord how thankful you are for your salvation and that He can use the power of His Holy Spirit to speak through you. Tell Him what's on your heart then wait for His peace and His still small voice to fill you with His love.

Week Eight, Day Three
Telling Others

It's easy to rejoice with the Samaritan woman. She was so transformed by her encounter with Jesus she actually did something remarkable.

> *Then, leaving her water jar, the woman went back to the town and said to the people, "Come, see a man who told me everything I ever did. Could this be the Messiah?" They came out of the town and made their way toward him* (John 4:28–30).

In her haste, the woman left her water jar. What a perfect picture that creates of leaving our old shame-filled life behind when we acknowledge Jesus Christ as our Savior. She personally knew the Messiah, the One who changed everything.

Consequences

It's important to remember, though, that God's forgiveness doesn't negate consequences of sin. We might be forgiven but still suffer the consequences of sinful choices. Paul reminded the believers in Philippi that he chose to persevere no matter what he had to confront. An attitude of perseverance is helpful when we have to work through results of prior choices.

> ...I press on to take hold of that for which Christ Jesus took hold of me. Brothers and sisters, I do not consider myself yet to have taken hold of it. But one thing I do: Forgetting what is behind and straining toward what is ahead, I press on toward the goal to win the prize for which God has called me heavenward in Christ Jesus (Phil. 3:12–14).

No doubt this woman sprinted into town. She had a message to proclaim!

> Many of the Samaritans from that town believed in him because of the woman's testimony, "He told me everything I ever did." So when the Samaritans came to him, they urged him to stay with them, and he stayed two days. And because of his words many more became believers.
>
> They said to the woman, "We no longer believe just because of what you said; now we have heard for ourselves, and we know that this man really is the Savior of the world" (John 4:29–42).

I want to emphasize the villagers' statement, "*We no longer believe just because of what you said; now we have heard for ourselves, and we know that this man really is the Savior of the world.*" Each person must make up their own mind. We can't "inherit" our faith from our parents or grandparents. Responding to the truth of Jesus, the Son of God, who died for the sins of the world, is an individual responsibility. What joy to see that truth expressed as this powerful story draws to a close.

Tomorrow we'll finish by examining the discussion Jesus had with his disciples after His encounter at the well.

Jot It Down

- Romans 10:9 is a helpful passage to share when speaking of Jesus and salvation. *If you declare with your mouth, "Jesus is Lord," and believe in your heart that God raised him from the dead, you will be saved.* Spend some time reflecting on this verse then write your thoughts as you consider its principles and your own salvation experience.

Week Eight, Day Four
The Big Picture

Review the "woman at the well" story in John 4 one more time paying particular attention to the disciples and their response when they return.

> *Meanwhile his disciples urged him, "Rabbi, eat something."*
>
> *But he said to them, "I have food to eat that you know nothing about."*
>
> *Then his disciples said to each other, "Could someone have brought him food?"*
>
> *"My food," said Jesus, "is to do the will of him who sent me and to finish his work"* (John 4:31–34).

The disciples had food on their minds. One of the responsibilities of disciples was to take care of their teacher. It's a teaching moment for Jesus as He reminds them of His number one priority, doing the Father's will. We find this in John 5:36 also. *...For the works that the Father has given me to finish—the very works that I am doing—testify that the Father has sent me.* Jesus now begins to instruct them in a

96

much bigger picture of His ministry and in what would one day be their own ministry.

> "*35*Don't you have a saying, 'It's still four months until harvest'? I tell you, open your eyes and look at the fields! They are ripe for harvest. *36*Even now the one who reaps draws a wage and harvests a crop for eternal life, so that the sower and the reaper may be glad together. *37*Thus the saying 'One sows and another reaps' is true. *38*I sent you to reap what you have not worked for. Others have done the hard work, and you have reaped the benefits of their labor."

When Jesus said, "*Open your eyes and look*," He wanted the disciples to become sensitive and alert to ministry moments/assignments themselves. The woman had transformed into a harvester when she ran into the village. The residents would soon arrive to see Jesus—the crop was ripe for harvest!

Shirley's Snippets

> I'd spent weeks meeting with a woman who wanted to know more about Jesus and the Bible. I enjoyed our time together as I sowed the seeds of the message of salvation into her life and watering it each week. To my surprise, another woman had the privilege of leading her to Christ. After a wave of jealousy, I remembered the body of Christ works together in sowing, watering and harvesting. The work is the Lord. Leave the outcome to Him.

Using Our Influence

The woman at the well probably never thought about having influence. She'd lived as a shameful social outcast in their culture due to her life choices. What mattered most to her was that she had met her Savior, and she told anyone who would listen. What courage! You, too, can find courage in Christ.

As Jesus left this earth after His resurrection, He left final instruction for the disciples and those who would believe because of them: "*Therefore go and make disciples of all nations, baptizing them in the name of the Father and of the Son and of the Holy Spirit, and teaching them to obey everything I have commanded you. And surely I am with you always, to the very end of the age.*" (Matthew 28:19-20).

Would you courageously ask Jesus to give you the opportunity to have a ministry moment, an assignment? It's the next step of growing as a disciple! May the Lord Jesus Christ find us faithful as we grow into abiding, fruitful, proven disciples. If we don't meet in person in this earthly life, I eagerly await hearing your stories in heaven!

You are loved!

Shirley Moses

Leader's Guide

The Content

All of Me provides an eight weeks Bible study designed to assist the new believer in becoming a committed disciple of Jesus Christ. Older Christians who have remained on the fringes of commitment will begin to understand what it means to follow Christ as a disciple. The guide includes resources for one-on-one discipleship or small group discipleship.

The Discipleship Mentor

A discipleship mentor should have been a believer for at least three years and is growing in her relationship with the Lord. She should be actively involved in her local church and in studying God's Word. She should also be seeking to live a life of integrity and commitment as she lives out God's love to those around her.

The Disciple

All of Me is written for any Christian woman who wants to grow in their understanding of what Christ is asking of them as His follower. Meeting with each member individually before the study begins will help determine if the disciple understands the commitment expected of her.

The Goal

Eight weeks of study and interaction with the Discipleship Mentor or small group leader allows participants time to experience what they're learning. It will also allow the relationship between the mentor and the leader to mature.

The Small Group Leader

Perhaps several women have asked to be discipled, which means you automatically have a small group. These resources will assist you in the time you spend together. Another option is temporarily dividing a large group already in place, like a Sunday morning Bible study, into small groups of three to four. In this case, using the application form will provide additional information useful for placing participants into respective groups. Trust God to reproduce His heart in their lives as you pray over them while sharing God's Word and His love.

Meeting Format

1. Open with prayer.
2. Read the primary Scripture passage.
3. Review their journaling contents.
4. Utilize resource questions as you choose.
5. Discuss one "take away" truth from each participant.
6. Preview the upcoming week.
7. Limit the meeting to one hour unless a longer time has been decided upon jointly.

Week One

The goal of this week is to understand salvation and to reflect upon their individual salvation experience with the desire to share it with others.

Day One:

- Discuss the benefits of using an outline to study a passage of scripture.
- Have them read or tell her salvation story.

Day Two:

- Look up and discuss Jeremiah 1:5; Ephesians 1:4; 1 Peter 2:9.
- Discuss the topic of rebirth to evaluate their understanding.
- Answer any questions that come up about baptism.
- Share a personal experience about releasing control to God.
- Additional verses for consideration: Mark 1:8; Luke 3:16.

Day Three:

- Discuss Nicodemus' questions of Jesus.
- Discuss Jesus' explanation/responses to Nicodemus.
- Ask who brings us to understand truth? (1 Corinthians 2:4)

Day Four:

- Discuss what Joseph and Nicodemus later did for Jesus.
- Ask about any resistance they might have from others in their choice to follow Jesus. Take time to pray for those mentioned.
- Discuss ministry options you might share together. (Visit a sick friend, deliver a meal, etc.)
- **Preview**: Next week we'll study about the Good Shepherd and what it means to trust Him to lead us.

Week Two

The goal this week is for the disciple to choose to follow Jesus and experience His protection, His fellowship, His provision and His purpose for her life.

Day One:

- Review the passage outline and anything the participant might have recorded in the Jot It Down section.
- Share a personal example of a time you were led astray by your deceitful heart.
- Ask if they want to discuss further the dependence/attitude the sheep needs to have.

Day Two:

- Discuss different places you have lived and the impact of these communities on your faith.
- Ask if they need clarification on any of the scriptures covered on Day Two.
- Share how you've learned to trust God's love even in difficult circumstances.
- Discuss a particular fear you've had to overcome. Ask if there are fears she currently faces.

Day Three:

- Share a personal "snippet" of how you learned the responsibility that comes with freedoms.
- Discuss the spiritual meaning of "the abundant life" in contrast to the abundance of things of the world and your own path of discovering the abundant life.

Day Four:

- Ask for examples of how God has provided in their life. Help them recognize the small things He has done for them.
- Discuss consequences of wrong choices and the pressure we face daily from culture.

- Read together 1 John 2:5 and ask them to explain the benefits of making the right choices.
- **Preview:** Next week you'll begin examining character traits that begin developing in the lives of disciples. The first one is "love."

Week Three

This week's goal is a fuller understanding of God's love and how a disciple shows that love through her life.

Day One:

- Review the passage outline. Ask for their thoughts on using an outline.
- Ask them to share a time God revealed His love in a personal way.

Day Two:

- Ask for their definition of "pride."
- Discuss the subtlety of pride and the variety of ways it shows up.
- Share personal examples of struggles with pride.

Day Three:

- Interact over the pattern Jesus established for restoring a relationship:

  1. Accept any personal responsibility.
  2. Acknowledge your underlying motives.
  3. Accept forgiveness.
  4. Accept directions from Jesus to move forward.
- Offer your confidence in their ability to work with God to restore any broken relationship in her life.

Day Four:

- Review examples she wrote down of how she demonstrates various qualities of love found in 1 Corinthians 13.
- **Preview**: You'll learn how our relationship with Jesus impacts our relationship with others.

Week Four

This week's goal guides disciples to develop loving acceptance and to extend mercy in her personal relationships.

Day One:

- Review the passage outline and anything from their journaling or Jot It Down notes.
- Discuss peer pressure and its influence on our behavior.

Day Two:

- Ask if she has ever been falsely accused or publicly embarrassed. A word of caution. Keep your response focused on biblical principles and how God has worked in the incident. Ask her to limit the specific details.

Day Three:

- Ask if she needs to talk through challenges in any personal relationship. Guide the conversation away from becoming too transparent and make sure you encourage her to allow the Shepherd to guide her in this relationship.

Day Four:

- Discuss the diversity of people God puts in our lives and what principles we can draw from the way Jesus related to someone so very different from Himself.

- **Preview**: Next week you'll focus on the importance of prayer in the life of a disciple.

Week Five

The goal of this week is to help the disciple recognize God's involvement in her life and to develop a prayer life that reflects her increasing realization of His presence and protection.

Day One:

- Review the outline and notes in Journaling Growth.
- Discuss how disciples can bring God glory as a result of difficult experiences.

Day Two:

- Talk about praying for protection for loved ones and if she would like for you to join her in praying for a specific person's protection.
- Discuss ways to pray for someone.

Day Three:

- Discuss the six ways Paul prayed for the believers in Philippi.
- Decide together which resource to use to pray for persecuted believers.

Day Four:

- Investigate their understanding of Paul's "ifs" in Philippians 2.
- Discuss examples of unity among believers.
- **Preview**: Next week you'll learn how the Holy Spirit works in a believer's life.

Week Six

Goal: This week the disciple will examine how to trust in Jesus' provision of comfort, peace and the Holy Spirit.

Day One:

- Review the passage outline and Jot It Down sections.
- Ask if they have any questions about Judas' betrayal.
- Ask her to share her thoughts in response to John 14:2, 3.

Day Two:

- Discuss any questions they might have about the Holy Spirit.
- Have her share something from her Jot It Down notes.

Day Three:

- See if your disciple can name all three persons of the Trinity and how they work to grow us into disciples.

Day Four:

- Have your disciple discuss her understanding of the Biblical phrase, "peace that passes understanding."
- Share a time when God brought you peace.
- **Preview**: Next week we'll be discussing how yielding your life as a disciple results in bearing spiritual fruit.

Week Seven

The goal of this week guides the believer to evaluate whether she's living a fruitful life based on John 15:1–8.

Day One:

- Review the outline and Journaling Growth notes.

- Ask her to explain her relationship to the True Vine and her understanding of the concept of pruning. Offer guidance if she is unsure.
- Read Luke 22:31, 32 together and have her share what failing Christ looks like in a disciple's life. Perhaps share a personal example to share.

Day Two:

- Ask her about ways believers stay connected to the vine.
- Point out areas of growth you see in her and fruit God is already producing in her life.

Day Three:

- Ask her to reflect upon a time when she first noticed growth/ fruit in her life.
- Clarify any additional questions she might have about how the Holy Spirit produces fruit.

Day Four:

- Ask your disciple to comment on this: "The more the Holy Spirit aligns our lives with His Word, the more our prayers will align with the Father's will—and fruit appears through our prayers."
- **Preview:** Next week we'll be discussing sharing our personal faith in Jesus Christ with others.

Week Eight

This chapter equips the disciple to have a confident answer concerning her relationship with Jesus and how to communicate the hope within her.

Day One:

- Review the outline and Journaling Growth notes.

- Discuss Peter's admonition in 1 Peter 3:15 to always be ready.
- Share a personal example of how you have learned to respond to someone's harsh response to sharing Christ.
- Have your disciple practice her brief testimony with you.

Day Two:

- Discuss the idea of directing a conversation to spiritual things when speaking with someone who is not a Christian. Perhaps role-play several scenarios.

Day Three:

- Offer to pray with her about anything else in her life that she would like to discuss with you.

Day Four:

- Decide if you would like to continue to be available to your disciple for future conversations about discipleship. If so, discuss your availability with her.

Additional Helps

- Listen with an open mind and heart.
- Anything shared in confidence must remain confidential
- Strive to keep the conversations "on track" and be intentional about covering the main points for that week.
- Try to meet at the same place each week for continuity. Be respectful of each other's time commitment.
- You are not expected to counsel or attempt to address any deep-seated problem. Some situations might require professional assistance. Your commitment is to share God's Word and to pray for her.
- Prayer is an essential part of each week's preparation.

- Consider compiling your favorite resources for growing spiritually and share them with your disciple.

Treasures for Your Heart

D isciples will always find themselves needing to know Scripture, not only for themselves, but also to pass along to others. Scripture provides instruction, comfort, conviction and protection of our minds, not only from the evil of our own hearts, but also from the devil himself. I believe you'll find the memorization of the following Scriptures worthwhile as you grow in your relationship with God.

The Disciple's Call

Chapter One

"Anyone who believes in Him is not condemned, but anyone who does not believe is already condemned, because he has not believed in the name of the one and only Son of God" (John 3:18).

The Disciple's Path

Chapter Two

"A thief comes only to steal and to kill and to destroy. I have come so that they [all believers] may have life and have it in abundance" (John 10:10).

The Disciple's Devotion

Chapter Three

"...He [Peter] said, 'Lord, you know everything! You know that I love You.' 'Feed My sheep,' Jesus said" (John 21:17).

The Disciple's Character

Chapter Four

"When they [the Pharisees] persisted in questioning Him, He stood up and said to them, 'The one without sin among you should be the first to throw a stone at her'" (John 8:7).

The Disciple's Confidence

Chapter Five

"I pray not only for these [His disciples], but also those who believe in Me through their message" (John 17:20).

The Disciple's Comfort

Chapter Six

"Peace I leave with you. I give to you. I do not give to you as the world gives. Your heart must not be troubled or fearful" (John 14:27).

The Disciple's Fruit

Chapter Seven

"My Father is glorified by this: that you produce much fruit and **prove** [emphasis mine] to be My disciple" (John 15:8).

The Disciple's Commitment—*All of Me*

Chapter Eight

"Listen [to what] I'm telling you: open your eyes and look at the fields, for they are ready for harvest" (John 4:35).

Disciple Application

Date: _____

Name: _____

Birthday: _____

Age: _____

Address: _____

City: _____

Zip: _____

E-Mail: _____

Phone: _____

I am interested in: (Please list 1st and 2nd choice)

- Participating in a discipleship small group (weekly)
- Participating through a discipleship 1 on 1 (weekly)

Work outside the Home? Part-time or Full time

_____

_____

What time of day is best for you to meet? (List day and time preferences in order.)

_____

_____

_____

_____

Meeting location preference? (List preferences in order.)

- Church
- Near your home/work
- No preference

Hobbies and interests:

_____

_____

_____

_____

What Bible studies have you participated in?

_____

_____

_____

_____

In what areas would you like to grow spiritually?

_____

_____

_____

_____

Return completed application to:

_____

Mentor Application

Date: _____

Name: _____

Birthday: _____

Age: _____

Address: _____

City: _____

Zip: _____

E-Mail: _____

Phone: _____

I am interested in: (Please list 1st and 2nd choice)

- Participating in a discipleship small group (weekly)
- Participating through a discipleship 1 on 1 (weekly)

Describe any experience you have had in a teaching/discipling relationship.

_____

_____

_____

_____

What ministries have you been involved in?

_____

_____

_____

_____

Please share your expectations and hopes as you serve as a PD.

_____

_____

_____

_____

What Bible studies have you participated in?

_____

_____

_____

_____

How do you keep growing in your relationship with the Lord?

_____

_____

_____

_____

In what areas of your life can you see spiritual growth within the last year?

_____
_____
_____
_____

Meeting location preference? (List preferences in order.)

Church

At your home

Near your home/work

No preference

Explain briefly how you came to know Jesus Christ personally.

_____
_____
_____
_____

Hobbies and interests:

_____
_____
_____
_____

Return completed application to:

_____
_____
_____
_____